1.1.
The Apple Parents

Daddy Apple: Brandon Maggart

How far does the apple fall from the tree? Not far, in the case of Fiona, as she spawned forth from long branches of entertainers.

Roscoe Maggart, Jr. (better known as Brandon Maggart) was born on December 12, 1933, in Carthage, Tennessee. From his lineage, we find a Melungeon bloodline, which is a mixed ethnic group who most notably come from Appalachia.

"There's this thing called Melungeon that apparently we are [...] whatever happened, like, slave ships would crash or there'd be mutiny or whatever. And so the back

Mountain Tennessee people and these slaves would all live in these communities." [2]

– Fiona Apple

At an early age, Brandon dove headfirst into the arts. A stint singing with the Knoxville Symphony earned him the Grace Moore Award, allowing him to further study his craft in New York City. While there, he won the 1963 Theatre World Award for his role in the musical *Put it in Writing*. In 1970, his part in the Broadway production *Applause* was nominated for a Tony Award for Best Performance by a Featured Actor in a Musical.

"Growing up, a lot of it was following my father on the road when he was doing the burlesque show with Sherry Britton, who was one of the first black burlesque stars. So it was me and my sister and the strippers taking us to get M&M's from the machine. And I'm sure my dad had every single one of them." [3]

– Fiona Apple

His transition to mainstream television was effortless, and his list of credits is extensive. From 1969 to 1997, you'll find his name on many hit shows such as *Sesame Street, Who's the Boss, ER, Boy Meets World, The Sentinel, Ellen, Married with Children,* and *Murder, She Wrote,* to name very few. In 1980, he

when
a song
ends in a
minor key

THE COMPLETE BIOGRAPHY OF

FIONA APPLE

USING HER OWN WORDS

by jared woods

When a Song Ends in a Minor Key:
The Complete Biography of Fiona Apple Using Her Own Words
by Jared Woods
co-editing by Milz Dechnik
cover photo by Photo12
published by The Goat's Nest Publishing
ISBN 9798332405389
ASIN B0D821KMH7
JaredWoodsSavedMyLife.com

THIS BOOK IS PROUDLY WRITTEN BY A HUMAN WITHOUT THE USE OF AI

Dedicated to My Patreon Subscribers

Aaron, Adam, Ahmed, Ama & Ross, Ammr, Bert, David,
Diana, Dollkitten, Gee, Joanne, Kez, Lenka, Lonnie, Marcus,
Mark, Milz, Ryan, Tami, Tony, Wilmie, Xen

Thank You for Supporting a Starving Author

Join the team! *patreon.com/legotrip*

Contents

"*I extract the negative stuff. I put it in a thing and I bring out all the bad stuff. And I serve it up to everyone so that they'll give me attention. And it poisons everyone, so they only listen to it when they're in fucked-up places. And it's a good sign when they stop listening to me, because that means that they're not hurting themselves on purpose.*"[1]

– Fiona Apple

Introduction

Would it be too obvious to start this biography with an apple metaphor? Or perhaps no comparison is quite as fitting? Indeed, the poetics of the apple's image extends beyond merely a name, and such associations could be treated as divine play rather than coincidence

Take a moment to watch an apple gradually growing growing growing, learning to become what it was always meant to be, while bravely offering itself out into the bigger world. For some, this gift is a glorious sum of nutrients feeding a gap in their yearning stomachs. However, for others, the apple is bitter, hard to swallow, or even poisonous.

These polarised cries from both sides are a hefty weight to bear, and a tough skin forms the exterior. The apple is doing its best to protect itself from harm, yet is only a nibble away from exposing the soft flesh inside. In the case of Fiona's apple, there is an additional vulnerability, for here is someone who was plucked off the tree far too young, unripe, undeveloped, and forced to deal with the harsh hardships of reality long before any apple would be ready.

19 years old. That's the age at which Fiona became internationally famous. And, as is the viciously hungry nature of

the media, jaws quickly snapped chunks from her soul, spitting them out in pieces that relabeled her turmoil as that of an ungrateful brat. She tumbled as the poster child for emotional breakdowns and eating disorders. Her onstage outbursts and meltdowns were not documented as a person who needed help, but rather as sticky tabloid syrup to sell more pages. Like the Biblical story of Genesis, we never blame the snakes for the misshapen apple. We turn to the woman as the scapegoat.

In what would crush most of us to cider, Fiona stood her ground. She proved that one can be fragile but unmoveable simultaneously, never suppressing the tears, never covering up the bruises. Instead, Fiona used these inner turbulences as artistic flames to mould her weapons, absorbing the difficulties and utilising them to churn out a delicious sauce for the music landscape to enjoy.

When a Song Ends in a Minor Key is the complete biography of Fiona Apple. From her unfailing critically applauded albums to their long titles to the even longer gaps between release dates. From her unlikely choices of celebrity lovers to her complicated relationships with women. From the endurance test through which the industry has pushed and pulled her to how she has learned to rewrite the rules until they suit herself. We follow these paths using her own words taken from hundreds of interviews while analysing every seed within a discography where Fiona unreservedly has laid herself bare across her piano keys, inviting us to grow with her.

This book is for Fiona, the apple of our eyes. And it is for her fans, her army marching behind her with our assorted fruits lifted high above our heads, prepared to defend our hero artist against anyone who dares step in her way.

Part One
Fiona Apple McAfee-Maggart

also starred in two films, namely *Dressed to Kill* and *Christmas Evil*. But perhaps his most important role was as Lou Waters in the Showtime comedy *Brothers*. Running 115 episodes from 1984 to 1989, Brandon was nominated for the Best Actor in a Comedy Series Cable ACE award four times (1985, 1986, 1988, 1989).

"I met Kermit. My dad used to be on Sesame Street when it was still in black and white." [4]

– Fiona Apple

In his later years, Maggart has focused on painting as well as writing books and poems, which have been well received. However, his legacy will not be remembered in these mediums or even his contributions in front of the camera. Instead, it is his genetic bloodline that has impressively outgrown even his achievements.

Brandon Maggart married LuJan Hudson in 1955. Together, they had five children before their divorce in 1971. These kids were Jennifer, Spencer, Justine, Julienne, and Garett—no Fiona in sight. Not until we introduce Diane McAfee...

"I'm from the second family. I'm the last of seven children [...] but their mother has always been very inviting to us." [4]

– Fiona Apple

Mommy Apple: Diane McAfee

"I'm the only woman in my family who's not a dancer, which sucks." [5]

– Fiona Apple

Fiona's mother, Diane McAfee, was herself born from a descent of entertainers. Her parents were big band vocalist Johnny McAfee and dancer Millicent Green. Furthermore, Diane's mother's mother was a dancer, too. However, details about Diane's life are not well publicised and, indeed, appear only in documentation once Fiona enters the conversation.

Brandon Maggart and Diane McAfee met on the 1970 Broadway musical production of *Applause* (based on the 1950 comedy-drama *All About Eve*). Maggart played Buzz Richards, and McAfee played Eve Harrington. By the end of the musical tour, the two had fallen in love. Their unmarried relationship lasted from 1973 to 1980, bearing two daughters: Amber and, of course, the youngest of the entire clan, Fiona.

1.2.
The Apple Kids

With one sister and five step-siblings, the McAfee-Maggart children are a small army. Jennifer and Julienne Maggart live privately outside of the spotlight. Unfortunately, Justine Maggart passed away in 1985 at age 25 due to a car accident in Norwalk, Fairfield County, Connecticut.

The remainder of the team is part of the entertainment industry and warrants additional details.

Spencer Maggart

Born in Darien, Connecticut, in 1962, Spencer Maggart (also known as Brandon, Jr.) has made a small name for himself as an actor and director. His most notable performance is as a skinhead in the 1997 TV movie *Things That Go Bump*. However, it is his work with Fiona that raises his significance in this book, as he directed several of her music videos, which we shall discover later.

Garett Maggart

Born in Darien, Connecticut, in 1969, Garett Maggart followed the closest in his father's footsteps as a TV and movie actor. His impressive credits include the shows *Frasier, ER, Days of Our Lives*, and *CSI*. As their field is so similar, Garett and his dad, Brandon, often worked together on each other's shows. For example, in Brandon's show *Brothers*, Garett plays the pizza boy in Season 5, Episode 7, "Moving Out". Conversely, when Garett had top billing on *The Sentinel*, his father played Brother Marcus on Season 1, Episode 10, "Vow of Silence".

Maude Maggart

Born in Manhattan, NYC, in 1975, Amber is Fiona's only full sibling as they share the same mother. In her 20s, Amber changed her name to Maude as an honour to her father's mother's mother, Maude May Apple. She pursued a career in cabaret performance, with her Los Angeles debut in 2001 widely praised. Critic Les Traub claimed Maude was "destined to become a major cabaret star."

This proved true as she has gone on to win multiple awards including The Tony Award for Outstanding Achievement in Cabaret. With seven albums under her name, we can also hear her soothing vocals on various of Fiona's projects, which we shall cover as we get to them.

"My sister is just phenomenal. I don't think there is anyone like her." [6]

– Maude Maggart

Ladies and Gentlemen, Fiona Apple

Finally, the youngest of seven, Fiona Apple McAfee-Maggart, was born on September 13, 1977, in New York City.

"Years ago, my mom told me: 'We almost died when you were born. Both of us.' Two weeks before I was due, she and my father were fighting on the phone. He was in Boston, and they weren't very happy with each other. She told me: 'I was rearranging furniture, and I wanted him to be there so he could help me push the couch. I was just so mad, so I pushed it myself and felt something strange. I was kind of in pain for a couple of weeks.' Her peritoneum, which is the film that holds all of your organs together, had ripped just a little bit. I was a Caesarean baby, and the doctor who delivered me later told me, 'I opened your mother up, and you were right there.'" [7]

– Fiona Apple

When Fiona was four, her parents split, and she stayed with her mother and sister in Morningside Gardens, Harlem, NYC. A 24-year-old accountant–guitar player moved in as her mother's long-term boyfriend. His name was Robert but Fiona affectionately refers to him as "Bird Face". Still, Fiona hung out with her dad often enough, spending summers with him in Los Angeles, California.

"My dad and my mom were never married, but when they split up, my mom met a guy when I was four [...] they're very wonderful people, and there's lots of laughter in my home growing up. Also, lots of passion. Lots of, you know, screaming and fighting and crying and laughing." [8]

– Fiona Apple

Not to speed too far into the future, but Fiona's branch on the family tree ends here.

"I've never wanted kids." [9]

– Fiona Apple

Perhaps this is owed to how being Fiona Apple is a full time job in itself? In fact, Fiona has often spoken about the fascinating concept of "self parenting."

"I have a thing about wanting to learn about parenting myself [...] I tend to buy a lot of books about parenting [...] I think if

there's something, like, say I have a problem with a work ethic. And maybe if I read a book about the new way to teach your kid about how to form a good work ethic, maybe I can do that to myself." [10]

– Fiona Apple

1.3.
Student Life

St. Hilda's & St. Hugh's School

"All through my childhood I did a lot of lying in bed thinking up the perfect way to tell somebody off. I mean, what I really say is, 'Aaaaaaah, fuck you, fuck you, fuck you!' But that's not good literature." [11]

– Fiona Apple

Fiona attended the private Episcopal school St. Hilda's & St. Hugh's in West Harlem from the second to the ninth grade. The school is proud of Fiona's triumphs, but other celebrities were educated here, too, including actor Anthony Michael Hall (*Sixteen Candles, The Breakfast Club, Edward Scissorhands*) and orthopaedic surgeon Evan Flatow.

"I have really good memories of that school. I think it was a great place. Really small, and really a diverse group of kids. Lots of exchange students went there for some reason. It's an Episcopalian school, but nobody even knew what Episcopalian meant. I still don't know what Episcopalian means. We went to chapel every morning and had Eucharist every Wednesday. There were nuns that taught there, but, strangely, it didn't feel like it was a religious school." [12]

– Fiona Apple

Speaking of religion...

"I'm not religious or anything, but now when I'm sad, I do a lot of kneeling on the ground and thanking whatever. Just for me, to acknowledge something and make it physical so that it sets in. The thing I will say always is, 'Thank you for my problems and I send my love everywhere.' I am generalising. There are problems that just fucking suck and are terrible. But problems like being sad or

having your heart broken aren't any less valuable than happiness is. So when things are really bad, nowadays I recognise the value in it because I know it is going to make me appreciate happiness in the future way more." [13]

– Fiona Apple

"I made a religion for myself as a kid, but that's another story." [14]

– Fiona Apple

Back to school, and sadly, Fiona was bullied during this phase.

"They didn't fight me. They just insulted [me with] nicknames and [those names] follow you. It was just like 'witch' or 'dog'. Those were mine." [15]

– Fiona Apple

"Once kids say those things, you get pinned and there's nothing you can do about it. My mother would send me out of the house and I'd turn around and ring the doorbell until *she let me back in. I went into evaluation and they said, 'she has chronic kind of mood disorder.' The kids heard about that and made fun of me even more. 'Go on, I dare you, ask her if she's crazy!'"* [11]

– Fiona Apple

One noteworthy incident during this challenging period was when Fiona attempted to sit with the "cool kids" at lunch. They promptly rejected her. However, a slightly older girl interjected. Her name was Shameika, and she told Fiona that she "had potential."

"I have no memory of anybody ever getting in the way of somebody else being shitty to me, from when I was a kid to when I was an adult. Except for this one moment where this girl walking by saw something going on, and leaned down and said, 'Hey, why do you care about them? You have potential.' I got to carry that in my head my whole life. When there was nobody on my side, I was able to call up those words." [16]

– Fiona Apple

Over the years, Fiona often wondered if the Shameika memory was accurate. Of course, if you know, you know, but that's for a later chapter.

Alexander Hamilton High School

In the tenth grade, Fiona moved to LA to be with her dad. Here, she attended Alexander Hamilton High School, a much larger establishment with a far more extensive list of celebrity attendees. These include Shia LaBeouf, Nikki Reed, Michele Lee, Lizzy Caplan, Rita Hayworth, David Cassidy, Michelle Phillips (from the Mamas and the Papas), Ariel Rechtshaid, and Syd. The establishment also made the news when it was revealed someone shot a porno named *Revenge of the Petites* on campus.

"My dad lived in Venice, and I went out to spend a year to live with him, and I went to Hamilton High for one year, in California. That was an awful year. St. Hilda's goes from nursery to twelfth grade, and there were three hundred kids in the whole school. Hamilton had five thousand kids for high school. At St. Hilda's, that small amount of kids from all over the world, all different religions, and it wasn't ever an issue. Going out to LA [...] the quad was the most segregated place I had ever seen. I didn't

know where to go. It was a terrible year. I couldn't really find any friends that stuck." [12]

– Fiona Apple

As Fiona noted, she was at Alexander Hamilton High for her sophomore year only.

Dropping Out

After skipping school 100 times in a single year (as she claims), Fiona moved back to New York, attending the night school, Rhodes.

"Rhodes was ridiculous. There was maybe twenty kids that went there. It was the only place I could go to because by the time I realised I was miserable in California. I didn't have very good grades to begin with. It was hard to get into a school, and it was like, 'Oh, Rhodes'll take me.' Everybody that was at Rhodes was those kids that like no one else would take them. And all the teachers that worked there—it wasn't like they were bad teachers, but everybody that worked there they were doing it to get extra money. They were teaching a class at night, because they needed the money. Nobody was really invested in it at all; everybody kind of had to be there." [12]

– Fiona Apple

Life in Rhodes didn't exactly pan out, either.

"The classes were an hour and a half, and you'd have forty-five minutes, and then a fifteen-minute break, and then another forty-five minutes. On a fifteen-minute break, everybody would go outside and smoke pot. There was no second forty-five minutes ever, and you'd be sitting out on the stoop and the teachers would be like, 'Come back into class,' and you'd be like, 'Why?' It was that kind of place. And then they closed down." [12]

– Fiona Apple

Fiona bounced back to California and entered a home school named Poseidon.

"It was actually a school for people with emotional problems, and I was really lucky to get in." [12]

– Fiona Apple

But when she was required to take a driver's ed to graduate, she decided to drop out of the school system altogether.

"It was frustrating, though, because I got all my work done to graduate in two months, and then they were like, 'I'm sorry, you have to take driver's ed.' I just kind of went, 'Oh, forget it.' At that point, I had already made a demo tape. I was going to be signed to Sony, and I was like, 'Whatever.'" [12]

– Fiona Apple

Hang on, we're getting ahead of ourselves. Of course, the music is why we are here, but we cannot understand her artistic output without first exploring the demons weaving through the complex mind behind Fiona's songs. So let's rewind and go back through Fiona's timeline again, but this round, focusing on the trauma which, unfortunately, has already been written about everywhere else to death.

"[I'm] the patron saint of mental illness, instead of as someone who creates things." [1]

– Fiona Apple

Part Two
Mental Health Troubles

2.1.
Ripening Brain

"I was the person that would walk into the room, and you'd hear 'here comes Miss Sunshine'. I wasn't a terror, I just didn't like anybody. I didn't like anything. My stepfather, Robert, used to say that he should get me a t-shirt that says 'I hate' on the top and then I can just fill it in for the rest of my life." [17]

– Fiona Apple

Fiona's mind was always a bundle of wires, viewing the world through a slightly darker lens than her peers. However, Fiona's outlook took a particularly negative plunge during an incident that not only forever plagued her psyche but has also remained a primary talking point in every biographical write-up and interview ever since.

2.2.
The Sexual Assault Incident

TRIGGER WARNING: SEXUAL ABUSE

On the day before Thanksgiving 1989, a 12-year-old Fiona entered her Harlem building and made her way up the elevator to the apartment she shared with her mother and sister. It was a journey she made daily, but today would be different and scar her mentality (and her art) for the rest of her life.

A man followed her into the building. She noticed him with caution. He reminded her of Jimi Hendrix.

"Strangely, it hasn't ruined Jimi Hendrix for me." [1]

– Fiona Apple

She could hear him following her on the stairs, stopping by

the elevator on every floor, waiting for her to exit. When she finally reached her stop, she ran to her door, fumbling wit her keys, but she was not fast enough.

"I was unlocking the locks on the door when he came up. He told me that I was going to be killed. There was a knife to my throat, but my dog was barking inside the apartment, so he was afraid of going inside." [18]

– Fiona Apple

He raped her. Fiona kept quiet throughout the ordeal, distracting herself by listening to her dog on the other side of the door.

    After the man finished, he wished her a happy Thanksgiving and left. He was never caught.

"When I shut the door, I was like, 'That's what you're supposed to do. You have to pray for the people who hurt you.' But you can't stop at praying for them. You have to hold them responsible." [19]

– Fiona Apple

Whatever underlying intricacies Fiona had in her developing mind were permanently tangled from this day forward. To what end she owes her mental issues or even her creative voice to this one moment could never be accurately dissected, but the long-term effects were undeniable. Violent nightmares swarmed her slumbers. Her OCD flared up. Her eating habits altered. She became fearful of older men. And her art became her only escape where she could exorcise her emotions. To a very public forum, as it turns out.

"It's funny, because I don't think that I maybe would be here [without the rape]. But then again, I don't think I would need to be here." [20]

– Fiona Apple

"It's a boring pain. It's such a fuckin' old pain that, you know, there's nothing poetic about it." [21]

– Fiona Apple

"My problem was that I felt ashamed of feeling sad or angry. Now, I don't hide my vulnerability in my lyrics. There's no way I was going to get raped and not get something out of it. I learned about power and hope and forgiveness. I like who I am

now, and I wouldn't be who I am if that hadn't happened." [22]

– Fiona Apple

"Rape is the most humiliating thing that can be done to you. It's the most vulnerable that you can be. But once I realised that, I became a stronger person and faced all my fears. It's like, well, the worst has happened and I'm fine. Now, I feel like whatever I do, no one can hurt me. I cannot be violated, I cannot be humiliated, I cannot be disregarded, I cannot be disrespected. If I respect myself and believe in what I'm doing, no one can touch me." [23]

– Fiona Apple

"How much strength does it take to hurt a little girl? How much strength does it take for the girl to get over it? Which one of them do you think is stronger?" [24]

– Fiona Apple

2.3.
Fighting
Disorders

"No one's normal. There is no normal otherwise, we'd all be the same person. I was talking about that the other day with somebody, and they're like, 'Yeah, well, would you give up all of your kind of craziness to be normal? And would you give up all this stuff?' And, of course, the answer is no. But, then again, the only reason why all this stuff is so important to me is because I am crazy." [25]

— Fiona Apple

Fiona has struggled with many mental ailments through-out her life which were only exasperated by the rape. Her diagnoses included obsessive-compulsive disorder, depression, anxiety, and complex post-traumatic stress disorder, which manifested in an array of unwanted behaviours.

"The brain is just a machine that sometimes gets a little glitch. This is just something that got into a loop, and it's getting reinforced." [8]

– Fiona Apple

She suffered from night terrors. She was too terrified to go to school. Due to her OCD, Fiona would rollerskate around her kitchen 88 times (the number of keys on the piano) to feel better. And when she announced on a school trip that she planned to kill herself and take her sister, Amber, with her, people took notice.

"There seemed to always be some kind of rumour going on around about me. It was either that I was gonna kill myself or that I was dealing drugs." [8]

– Fiona Apple

She was sent for psychiatric evaluation and ended up in therapy, being told that she "thought too much".

"I've spent my whole life telling my innermost secrets to strangers." [24]

– Fiona Apple

"I remember I used to put a bra on over my shirt and then let go and just sit down and not say anything about it. Just to distract their attention. So the whole time they'd be, like, 'why is your bra over your shirt? This is hostile. Why are you doing this?' so that I wouldn't have to talk about things. Because I didn't really feel like I had anything to talk about." [27]

– Fiona Apple

"I don't get depressed and stay depressed for a long time. What would happen to me is the most exhausting thing. I wanted to die before. I truly did want to die before. I remember I would be sitting in my shrink's office, looking at his computer with one of those screensavers on, and they have all these cubes in different colours, and I swear

my mood would change. A purple square would come up, and I'd feel, 'Everything's OK,' then a green one would come up, and I'd be, 'Everything's terrible.' It would make no sense to me. I still don't understand it." [20]

– Fiona Apple

Her OCD continued to escalate into her adulthood.

"My main thing is faces. Seeing faces in my head while. I do certain things [...] I would always think of faces when I was doing something. Crossing a threshold in a room when I would turn on the shower. The water hits the floor of the shower. When I put shampoo in my hair. When the shampoo touches my hair, even when I watch my dog [...] the thing happens that it would make me have to repeat things if I see the wrong face [...] I would have to think of somebody else's face with who I was getting along." [28]

– Fiona Apple

Self-harm is another undesirable thread in Fiona's troubled manifestations. For example, she admitted to biting her lip as hard as possible.

> *"And it'll be bleeding, and I can't stop, because it almost feels so good when I bite my lip. It was never, like, 'I am going to hurt myself and put myself in the hospital.' It is that I am going to give myself the pain that I need to feel to put the punctuation on this shit that's going on inside."* [20]

– Fiona Apple

These self-harmful actions extend to scratching, where visible scars still reside on her arms.

> *"I have a little bit of a problem with that. It's a common thing. It just makes you feel."* [29]

– Fiona Apple

> *"Why should I hide shit? Why does that give people a bad opinion of me? It's a reality. A lot of people do it. Courtney Love pulled me aside at a party and showed me her marks."* [20]

– Fiona Apple

One of the most publicised results of her troubles was her weight loss, which Fiona explains was a result of her OCD.

"With food, it's more the colours of food. If things don't look right. You could call it an eating disorder, but it wouldn't be, because I wasn't trying to avoid foods that were fattening. It was because I couldn't either decide what to eat or the colour wasn't right of this thing. Something that was more fattening if it was right to colour... but they also have to be pure. I can't have too many ingredients. There's a picture of it in my head, and there's a picture of the day and the day as a shape and the colours as the shapes. It's an issue of, like, that's not the right shape or doesn't fit into the shape of the day that I have in my head. It needs to be that way." [28]

– Fiona Apple

"I couldn't eat things that looked a certain way, that were a certain colour. I mean, there was a time when I couldn't eat things that I felt clashed with what I was wearing. I don't mean 'clash' like 'fashionably clash'. There was just something in my head that if it didn't balance, I couldn't eat it, and I was so afraid of doing the wrong thing. If I ate something, I felt like I was doing it because I don't want to be crazy. 'I'm going to eat that fucking apple right now, even though I'm wearing a yellow dress.' This would go on in my head all the time. And it's exhausting. I would tell my sister, 'I'm just so tired I can't manage myself anymore.' I felt like I was the mother of some retarded child that was throwing fits all the time, and I couldn't help it. It would take me half an hour to pick an apple out of the drawer. I couldn't pick the right one. [It was] because I felt like I had no control over my life, and that was the only way for me to take control of." [20]

– Fiona Apple

Understandably, her eating disorder was directly related to her sexual assault incident.

"I definitely had an eating disorder. What was really frustrating for me was that everyone thought I was anorexic, and I wasn't. I was really depressed and self-loathing. For me, it wasn't about being thin; it was about getting rid of the bait attached to my body. A lot of it came from the self-loathing that came from being raped at the point of developing my voluptuousness. I just thought that if you had a body and if you had anything on you that would be grabbed, it would be grabbed. So I did purposely get rid of it." [22]

– Fiona Apple

Fiona has been prescribed various medications for her disorders but she is uncharacteristically private when it comes to the exact drugs. However, we do know she believes she was wrongly on antipsychotics for her night terrors. Thankfully, she has long since weaned herself off from those drugs.

"When you try to come off an antipsychotic, the withdrawal is much different than other medications. I was getting tics, and it was the worst. I woke up one day, and I couldn't

see. It was double vision from morning until night, and we found out that was a side effect from withdrawal. This is dangerous stuff." [30]

– Fiona Apple

2.4.
A Career in Self Defense?

"My mom was telling me, 'you should take a self-defense class', and I just couldn't. But I was going crazy because I couldn't come home without having a panic attack, right? And so I came out [to LA] for a year of school, so then finally I did take the self-defence class." [31]

– Fiona Apple

After the sexual assault incident, Apple attended Model Mugging. It is a self-defence program founded by Matt Thomas that trains the victim to turn their fear adrenaline re-action into an active fighting mode.

"I find that really if you get in a pinch, I really think that biting is the way to go." [31]

– Fiona Apple

Fiona got a lot out of the course, so much so that she contemplated turning it into a career.

"I took a self defense course, and I decided I wanted to teach classes." [31]

– Fiona Apple

"The class was five hours a day for five weeks [...], and we would learn how to fight all day with all these women and stuff. And it felt great! There was this woman, I can't remember her name, but she was like this beautiful woman. She was a young lady and she seemed like she had been doing this for just a little bit of time, but she was good. And she was special, and she and she was one of the teachers. And I was, like, I'm gonna be her." [31]

– Fiona Apple

Who knows where this pursuit may have ended, but we can be grateful that she ultimately stuck with Plan A: The Music.

Part Three
Musical Timeline

3.1.
What Do You Want To Be When You Grow Up?

"I like this about myself, actually. I think back to when I was a kid, I never worried about what I was gonna do. I never thought about it. I never thought to worry about not doing well in school. I understood what I was supposed to do, and I understood why and everything, but I just wasn't worried." [32]

– Fiona Apple

Despite being raised in the entertainment industry, young Fiona's future career was not immediately set in stone, even if the craft of writing always beckoned to her.

"I wrote short stories and stuff [...] I wrote so many declarations of things. I used to be so cool. I would think about big issues. I would, like, cut class, but I would go to the library, and I would read about stuff [...] and I would think about it, and then I would be up in my little loft bed late at night, and I'd be writing about my opinion about life after death or whatever. I'd just figure out what I knew about things because of quote books and philosophers. I thought that philosophers just come up with quotes, so I said I'm gonna be a philosopher. I wanna come up with quotes. Songs are pretty good for that." [33]

– Fiona Apple

"I can remember sitting at my desk in my room, up at my mom's house. And I remember my mom calling me for dinner over and over and over again, and me saying, 'Wait, wait, wait,' because I was writing a story. I wasn't going to leave until I was

finished because I really enjoyed writing the story. I always remember that: I wasn't going to go and eat dinner because I was finishing writing a story." [12]

– Fiona Apple

"I went to the library when I was a kid and I read all these poems in this book. And sometimes it says 'anon' because they don't know the poet. And I went home and told my mom that my favourite poet is Anon." [34]

– Fiona Apple

3.2.
Early Musical Sproutings

"When I look back, there have always been things to be thankful for. I got a lot of encouragement with my music. My parents did say I was very talented. It wasn't all horrible." [18]

– Fiona Apple

As an 8-year-old, Fiona asked her mother for piano lessons because she wanted "to make people happy." It didn't take long before her classical training was underway as she composed her own pieces while playing along with jazz classics.

"My mom used to say that when there was anything wrong with me that there would be three sounds. The first sound would be me stomping down a hall to my room. Then the door slamming. And then just all this banging on the piano." [35]

– Fiona Apple

"I took lessons briefly around 8, but I didn't like being told what to play. I enjoyed improvising. It was kind of an escape into my own little world." [18]

– Fiona Apple

"I had been playing piano very seriously starting when I was about eleven. I started out by writing scores to chase scenes in the National Geographic Explorer series. I would see a lion chasing an impala; the impala with those gorgeous jumps. I remember I would go into my room and try to make the jump happen on the piano, and the chase happen on the piano." [36]

– Fiona Apple

The compositions with lyrics came a bit later.

"My friend Manuela, who was my best friend in second grade, she had a huge fight with her parents. And it was just, like, 'oh well, what you do when your friend is upset? You write a song for them.' And so I wrote a song called 'Manuela' and that kind of started me writing songs with words." [36]

– Fiona Apple

Adorably, you can hear Fiona sing some of that very first song on YouTube. Search for the video *FIONA APPLE Citizens Arrest EP. 1*, it comes on around 7 minutes 39 seconds.

"I can remember coming home from school singing, and not because I was happy. I was actually pretty unhappy. It was just my way of dealing with things. [Music] became a place to put whatever anger or frustration. It's very selfish. I'm doing this for myself, absolutely." [37]

– Fiona Apple

"[I'd] just start singing and it would make me feel better. It would kind of flush out all my feelings." [38]

– Fiona Apple

3.3.
General Songwriting Quotes by Fiona Apple

A s the years rolled on, Fiona's love for piano songwriting flourished. These developments, combined with her unique mind, have led to many fascinating observations and perspectives, which we shall let her tell herself.

"There was always something that I was drawn to about the piano because of its percussive nature, you know? I guess in the same way that some people like to get their

aggression out by playing drums or hitting people. I like to hit the piano." [39]

– Fiona Apple

"The worst feeling in the world, and this has been happening since I was like eight years old, [is when] I would write little songs, and I would be so excited and I'd get like my mom to come in and listen to it. And as soon as I would be done playing the song I would get so depressed. I still don't understand. It's just like a letdown. I guess I expect somebody to hear it and then the world just becomes bigger and brighter all of a sudden because I've played this song out loud for the first time." [40]

– Fiona Apple

"I'm so happy with myself. I can read music, but really slowly, but I find it really relaxing and really great. It's like you're doing a long crossword puzzle when you can work it out on the piano for a classical piece. I like being able to play them, and I actually did that.

A year ago, I got a book of Schubert, and I found the one that was easiest, and I spent a few days, and I actually got it down." [12]

– Fiona Apple

"I really enjoy fitting words together, but I only enjoy it when it's kind of easy, when it just kind of rolls along by itself. I never erase or cross out anything. I hardly ever write anything down. The song will be completely written in my head before it's actually written down." [41]

– Fiona Apple

"I won't write a song unless it serves me in some way. Where I feel like I have to write the song to make myself feel better. You know, if you're not overflowing with something, then there's nothing to get." [42]

– Fiona Apple

"I don't really know that much about pianos [...] I have a great one. It's the piano in my house, and it's an upright and it's a Steinway—and I'm not one hundred percent sure that it's a Steinway—but I'm not really picky. My own piano, it's got a note that won't play now. I know I could get it fixed, and the pedal's all fucked up. I just haven't had anybody come in and do something to it, so there's just some things that are getting a little rickety in it." [12]

– Fiona Apple

"When I was a kid, I used to play piano every night. I used to go and sit at a piano, and it would be something that I loved to do. I hardly ever play piano anymore. For the past ten years I didn't play piano. And when I'm writing a song, I'll play piano for ten minutes at a time. Some days, I have a piano day, and some nights, I have a piano night. I'll just love it again, and I'll do it for a while, but it's very, very rare." [12]

– Fiona Apple

"I'm a fucking contradicting little kid most of the time, except in my songs. That's the only time I can actually focus and go, 'This is the truth about this. This is the way it is.' And then I write it down so that I can have it in my memory because as soon as I'm done, I'm going to start acting like an idiot again." [43]

– Fiona Apple

3.4.
Influencing Fiona

"I was into everything that I'm into now, which is basically everything except for like country and techno. I was listening to a lot of Billie Holiday and Ella Fitzgerald." [44]

– Fiona Apple

Fiona has never been shy to shout love for those artists who have shaped her style. Some names one may find regularly include Cyndi Lauper, Kate Bush, The Beatles, Harry Belafonte, Bob Dylan, Miriam Makeba, Alice Coltrane, Jimi Hendrix, Schubert, and Jack Teagarden.

Another fantastic way to pick out her favourites is to seek her live cover performances. Some of the best ones include "Angel" by Jimi Hendrix, "Sitting in Limbo" by Jimmy Cliff, "Use Me" by Bill Withers, "Kissing My Love" by Bill Withers, "Please Come Home for Christmas" by Charles Brown, "After You've Gone" by Marion Harris, and "Just One of Those

Things" by Frank Sinatra.

However, there are those names who rise even higher than others, such as Billie Holiday, Ella Fitzgerald, and Joan Armatrading.

"If I had to pick one record that's closest to me from when I was a kid, it's [Joan Armatrading's] To the Limit. I feel like it influenced me a lot [...] I love her singing style, I love her voice, I love the way she says things." [45]

– Fiona Apple

"[Joan Armatrading] was playing in New York, like, 10 or 15 years ago, an outdoor show down by one of the piers. I was just walking by, and I heard her, so I went, and I watched Joan Armatrading by myself. I tried to make a video when she started doing 'You Rope You Tie Me,' and I got tapped by the guard telling me to stop filming. At that moment, I felt such closeness and empathy for all the people I've seen at my shows getting told, 'Don't film that, don't

interrupt.' You're like, 'I'm sorry!' I felt
so ashamed." [45]

– Fiona Apple

"I'm telling you, I don't know shit about
music. My musical roots mainly come from
The Real Book. It's a book of jazz standards
I found at home on my mom's shelf, and on
each page it'd say, 'this is so-and-so's song
as sung by Billie Holiday or Ella Fitzgerald'.
I'd teach myself the songs without hearing
them, then I'd buy the albums and see if I'd
gotten it right." [46]

– Fiona Apple

And yet, it was someone outside of music that has appeared to
have a greater effect on Fiona than anyone else: the civil rights
activist author Maya Angelou.

"My mom gave me a compilation book
of [Maya Angelou's] poetry when I was
younger, and I was so impressed with who
she was. Just her as being her. But, I mean,
if you ever heard the woman speak, it's like
she's just she's so smart, and she's so well

grounded, and she has such a wonderful understanding and a beautiful perspective of the world that I just admired her so much. She is so honest and upfront and direct with the way that she feels about things. She was so open with her vulnerabilities and her weaknesses and then she was such a proud strong woman that I was very inspired by that. It gave me a lot of hope to think, well, I have these weaknesses too. I can be like that woman. I can be as proud and as strong and as wonderful as she is." [47]

– Fiona Apple

"There was just something in [Maya Angelou's] writing that I related to. You know, I spent so much time being ashamed of certain things about me. Being ashamed of being a very sensitive person because, you know, it's not cool to be sensitive. It's cool to be like, 'Nothing gets to me,' so I grew up just kind of feeling really ashamed of being sensitive. And when I would read everything *that she wrote, not just her poetry, but the books that she's written [...] it would give me a lot of hope just to read about somebody that I admired and to know that she had weaknesses. That she wasn't just a totally strong person born perfect like everyone else seems to be. I remember I used to look at the book on the back cover and, like, that woman. You can see it like in her posture and in her eyes and in her smile that she knows who she is and she's proud of who she is. And to know that she had been through similar things that I've been through, it was an incredible hope for me."* [48]

– Fiona Apple

Of course, as the media likes to do, Fiona was often compared to other outspoken female artists such as Nina Simone, Joni Mitchell, and Laura Nyro. There were plenty of contemporary examples, too, such as Courtney Love, Tori Amos, and, perhaps most frequently, Alanis Morissette.

"Alanis broke the ceiling, and then I walked into an office and they said, 'Girl... young... songwriter... sign here." [20]

– Fiona Apple

The only one who appeared to not pay any attention was Fiona herself.

> *"I heard about [Alanis] for the first time while I was tracking my record."* [49]
>
> ## – Fiona Apple

> *"I can explain that right here, right now. Alanis: we're both white, have long hair parted down the middle, and we're young people who get angry sometimes. It ends there. Tori Amos, two words: piano, rape. They're unintelligent comparisons."* [46]
>
> ## – Fiona Apple

> *"I have no sense of what gets on radio or MTV. I have not listened to those kinds of radio stations, or I have not watched any MTV or anything in years."* [12]
>
> ## – Fiona Apple

That is not to say Fiona has zero clue about what was running through the music bloodstream, and she has shown her support for fellow female musicians. A good example would be

Sinéad O'Connor, after she tore up a photograph of Pope John Paul II on Saturday Night Live in 1992.

"I heard about the pope thing, and I really don't know anything about him. He may be a wonderful man, and [Sinéad] may be completely wrong, but I love [Sinéad] anyway for doing what she believes in. Not all of us are there as just background music. Some of us are there to say something." [18]

– Fiona Apple

For extra fun times, search for *Fiona Apple appreciates Sinead O'Connor Mandinka* on YouTube.

"Hello, Sinead O'Connor. I'm Fiona Apple. I want you to know that you are my hero." [50]

– Fiona Apple

3.5.
First Demo

"I had this incredibly strong intuition. I told my sister that I'd heard a voice telling me to go to California and make a demo tape because all of a sudden, this clarity came to me. Because this was the time of my life when I was supposed to start having one of those identity crisises. Like, 'What am I gonna do with my life?' and everything. And all of a sudden, I realised, wait, you shouldn't really worry about it. Just have the clarity and have the vision to see which doors are opening for you and follow that way. And for some reason, it just felt like California meant, to me, show business. California meant, go out there and record and do your music things. That's what my dad always wanted me to do. And I was like, I think I've to go do this." [51]

– Fiona Apple

With nudges from her father, Fiona visited a recording studio in Venice called Mad Dog Studios (later Stanley Studios) in 1994. Costing $1,500 for three days, they came out the other side with three songs to tape.

"I had been hearing her songs since she was 11 or 12, and we used to even make little homemade tapes. To me, the songs were exceptional, never just little kid things. They really told what it felt like to be growing up." [18]

– Brandon Maggart, Fiona's Dad

"The next summer, she came back—she had trouble sleeping at night—and she had written these inaccessible lyrics about darkness. It kind of scared me in the beginning." [20]

– Brandon Maggart, Fiona's Dad

Two of these demo songs remain unreleased and unheard, namely "Not One of Those Times" and "He Takes a Taxi".

"There's two songs on it [...] that are bad." [52]

– Fiona Apple

However, the "Never Is a Promise" track was deemed good enough to rerecord for later projects, as we shall see.

"If I were to hear it again now, I think I would really hate it. I had been writing songs, and they were all kind of sad, and so I wanted to write a happy song, and the only way that I could figure out how to write lyrics that were happy was that I could write about feeling really bad and then say, 'This is not one of those times.' That was my only way of making it happy, because I didn't know how to say a happy thing at the time." [12]

– Fiona Apple

Armed with an armful of demo copies, Fiona was made aware of the next steps involving the gruelling nature of the entertainment industry. She didn't feel up for the task.

"We made up our first batch of tapes with 78 tapes, and I thought that was a ridiculous amount of tapes to make up because I just wasn't willing to talk to that many people about the music." [53]

– Fiona Apple

"My dad said we're gonna have to send out copies all over the place. 'You're gonna have to hand them out on the street.' [...] He was saying that it was gonna take years. I was gonna meet five or six managers before I found the one that I wanted to stay with. That I was gonna have to send them to every A&R guy on the planet and wait. And I really was not gonna do that. I wasn't gonna go play clubs either, and I'm in complete awe of the bands that do that for years and years waiting for a record deal." [51]

– Fiona Apple

Lucky for her, she didn't have to, as her story unfolded far quicker and uncomplicated than almost any other success story you're likely to hear.

"*I never even got to the place where I was going to make an effort.*" [54]

– Fiona Apple

3.6.
Sony Comes Knocking

"I've been around my family, and so many show business people all of my life. I didn't need anybody to tell me, 'Hey, you know, kid, you only get one chance' or something. And people would come up to me when I was, like, 11 to try to do something with MTV. And I'd said, no, I'm not ready yet. But this time, I thought... I don't think it's going to happen again." [55]

– Fiona Apple

With 78 demo tapes ready to go, Fiona Apple got to work by handing out one single copy to her friend, Anna.

The immediate chain reaction eradicates the accepted idea that becoming a signed artist has to be a difficult ordeal.

"I gave one to my friend, and she was babysitting for Kathryn Schenker, who is a publicist. Kathy had a party, and [Andy Slater] went to the party and called me up." [53]

– Fiona Apple

Andy Slater was a producer, manager, and Sony Music executive. He is known for his work with The Wallflowers, Dave Navarro, Stevie Nicks, Macy Gray, OK Go, Lisa Marie Presley, and Lenny Kravitz. Fiona's song "Never Is A Promise" snatched his attention, and he sought to meet her immediately.

"I wrote the songs that were on my demo, and I brought them to Andy Slater. I was expecting that I was going to know somebody who they would give my songs to. The first thing he said was, 'Well, first of all, you have a beautiful voice', and I'll remember that forever. Because I was like... I do?" [5]

– Fiona Apple

Slater passed the tape to Jeff Ayeroff and Jordan Harris, who led WORK Records, a Sony Music division. And together, they signed her up within seconds.

"The truth is we signed her before we ever met her. We just fell completely in love with the music." [18]

– Jeff Ayeroff, Record Executive

"There's no showbiz artifice in her. She's honest, and when you interview her, you get what she is on the day she shows up." [24]

– Andy Slater, Producer/Manager

"So I still have, you know, 77 tapes." [54]

– Fiona Apple

3.7.
An Apple by Any Other Name Would Taste as Sweet

"Everyone has always worried that people are taking advantage of me. Even the people who take advantage of me worry that people are taking advantage of me." [1]

– Fiona Apple

Fiona was seventeen when she signed on Sony's dotted line, meaning her mother had to co-sign the contract. And then it came time to decide on her name, as Fiona McAfee-Maggart was perhaps too clunky for showbiz. Her mother tried to help.

"She phoned up and said, 'I've got a great name! You know how you're always alone? You could call yourself Fiona Lone.'" [20]

– Fiona Apple

"Fiona Maria" was also seriously considered, but there was just one name Fiona did *not* want.

*"I remember meeting people from Sony and them being, like, 'What do you want your name to be?' And I was, like, **not** Fiona Apple. It's too obvious."* [56]

– Fiona Apple

"Apple is my middle name, and it was my grandmother's last name, I think. I guess my mom just let my dad believe that she was gonna call me Apple after his grandmother, but in truth, it was because my mom's best friend had a daughter and gave her daughter the middle name Orange. So, it turns out I'm just named after a fruit." [57]

– Fiona Apple

"Then six months later, the contract comes. 'Your stage name is Fiona Apple'. I started laughing." [20]

– Fiona Apple

Part Four
Tidal

4.1.
Album: Tidal (1996)

1. Sleep to Dream (4:08)
(second single)
2. Sullen Girl (3:54)
3. Shadowboxer (5:24)
(first single)
4. Criminal (5:41)
(third single)
5. Slow Like Honey (5:56)
6. The First Taste (4:47)
7. Never Is a Promise (5:54)
8. The Child Is Gone (4:14)
9. Pale September (5:50)
(featuring Maude Maggart)
10. Carrion (5:43)

TOTAL RUNTIME: 51:31

"When I did Tidal, it was more for the sake of proving myself. Telling people from my past something. And to also try to get friends for the future." [58]

– Fiona Apple

On July 23, 1996, Work Records and Columbia Records released Fiona Apple's debut. Recording bounced around assorted Los Angeles studios, including Sony, Ocean Way, and 4th Street, with Andrew Slater behind the production desk. Session musicians included drummer Matt Chamberlain (Pearl Jam, David Bowie, Tori Amos, Elton

John, Lisa Marie Presley, Garbage), bassist Sara Lee (Gang of Four, B-52s, Indigo Girls), guitarist Greg Leisz (The Bangles, Eric Clapton, Haim, Joni Mitchell, Bruce Springsteen, to name a few!), and keyboardist Patrick Warren (Stevie Nicks, Bob Dylan, Lana Del Rey). But above everyone would be multi-instrumentalist Jon Brion, who is so important to the Fiona story that we shall revisit his name throughout.

"She had never played with other musicians when we started cutting the album. She didn't have all the songs written, and for a long time it was just me trying to find out what kind of sound she liked—Ella Fitzgerald, Billie Holliday, and the hip-hop records. So we started from there." [24]

– Andy Slater, Manager/Producer

Like every album, Fiona wrote all of the songs herself.

"I'm not [picking on] Christina Aguilera, because it seems like she can sing, but I was reading that the people who wrote her 'Genie in a Bottle' song said something to the effect of, 'It was really great she could sing. We didn't have to use any pitch control.' And it makes me feel like, okay, if this is

credit that she's gotten for not having to use pitch control, then I want fucking extra, extra, extra credit! But not only do I not get extra credit for writing things, it's not even something that anyone's interested in." [43]

– Fiona Apple

Title

Fiona unleashed her heart to tape with songs primarily focused upon the breakup with her first boyfriend, Tyson. The visual of tidal waves appeared to perfectly encapsulate the turbulence of relationships, but as it turns out, the chosen word was not quite as clever as we'd assume.

"I never thought that there was much point in having a title to an album anyway. There was not a theme to my album, it was just kind of a bunch of songs that I threw together. So it was making fun of the fact that it was supposed to be Title, and I was going to call it Title. And then it turned into just being like about the fact that whole album is just kind of up and down and all

the, you know, roller coaster of me and my sick emotional weirdness and all that." [59]

– Fiona Apple

Sound

"It was hard to have to get on your toes about stuff, and be, like, well, that thing that I was going to finish in the next 10 years, I guess I have to finish it by Saturday." [60]

– Fiona Apple

Tidal's sound has been described as piano rock meets chamber pop, with occasional nods to jazz and art pop.

"The whole time, I was saying, 'But I don't want to play piano on this. I only wrote songs on the piano because it's the only instrument I know. I don't want this to be a fuckin' piano album.' But Andy kept saying, 'No, this is how you sound. This is you." [61]

– Fiona Apple

Artwork

"If you want to see me cry, come to a photo shoot. They treat me like I'm a hotel room." [62]

– Fiona Apple

Work Group record executive Jeff Ayeroff is reportedly the man behind the artwork. He concentrated on Fiona's eyes to capture the sombre mood of her musical personality. The fact that her features were so aesthetically pleasing probably nudged the direction, too.

"I knew the drummer who worked on the demos who told us she was beautiful and not to worry. I had somebody check it out. I didn't sign her thinking she weighed 400 pounds." [49]

– Jeff Ayeroff, Record Executive

"I liked the photos, but then when I saw the finished CD, I had been totally airbrushed. I just hated that, how it looked all slick." [43]

– Fiona Apple

Charts

"I'm impressed with myself for getting here, but I'm not so impressed with here." [63]

– Fiona Apple

Whatever anyone thought or didn't think, *Tidal* worked, hitting #2 on the US Heatseekers Albums charts and reaching the top 25 on the US Billboard 200 (15), in France (21), and in New Zealand (22). *Tidal* achieved platinum status within the year, and two decades later, it had sold 2.9 million copies, certified three times platinum in the US.

"It was a tough time, and I don't think that I ever want to revisit that kind of popularity. It hurts your feelings. It hurt my feelings, to be misunderstood, to be talked about." [64]

– Fiona Apple

Critical

Critical acclaim was even more remarkable. LA Times gave it three stars out of four, prophetically musing, "Just think of how formidable she'll be with a few more years of troublemaking under her belt." With a nine out of ten, Pitchfork said, "Fiona

Apple grapples eloquently with isolation, retribution, and the oceanic ups and downs of being young and being a woman. Rare is a debut so fully formed." The record is included in the book *1001 Albums You Must Hear Before You Die*, while Rolling Stone later claimed it as the 83rd Greatest Album of the 1990s and the 25th Best Debut Album of All Time.

Conversely, and strangely, Rolling Stone's initial reaction was lukewarm at best, calling it "seductively miserable" with a 6/10 score, while The Sydney Morning Herald claims "she reverts to gender cliche" with 5/10. Even worse, Fiona was more likely to agree with the negatives.

"I have a fucking huge memory of just hating all the songs on the last album when we were finishing it. A lot of that record was me going, 'I don't know, what do you think is better? Go ahead.' It just sounds a little bit undecided. I didn't know enough." [43]

– Fiona Apple

Singles

• Shadowboxer

Released July 1, 1996, "Shadowboxer" was the album's lead single. As expected, the critics worshipped the song, with Entertainment Weekly noting she sounds "like Nina Simone covering early Elton John. Although she's only 18, she has the poise of a seasoned singer." AllMusic used the word "haunting" to describe it. Sales were also respectable, hitting #32 and #34 on the US Adult Top 40 and US Alternative Airplay charts, respectively.

"It was because of this guy I had gone out with and had been really, really close with. I really loved him. I felt that he was my best friend. But he was a teenage guy, and they don't think a lot of times. He mistreated me, and then he came back. I couldn't even be friends with him for a while. I cared about him, but it was just a situation where he kept trying to be friends with me, but I knew that he just wanted to be friends with me so he could have the option of making a move on me whenever he wanted to. And because I was so infatuated with him, and even in love with him, I was always available for that. It made me feel weak every time I would fall for that. And I would look forward to him making a move on me, but I knew that it was wrong. I knew that he was playing with me. And after a while, I didn't *even care anymore because I wanted him so much.*" [65]

– Fiona Apple

The simplistic black-and-white music video was shot in the recording studio, where we see Fiona singing into a microphone and playing her piano. Later that year, Fiona performed the song on Season 22, Episode 6 of *Saturday Night Live*, hosted by Robert Downey Jr.

• Sleep to Dream

"Sleep to Dream" was the second single, coming out quite a while later, on April 14, 1997. The song title was one of Fiona's first-ever lyrics.

"I started writing it when I was fourteen. It's about an asshole. An old boyfriend." [46]

– Fiona Apple

Hitting #28 on the US Alternative Airplay chart, Time and People magazine called the song "smouldering." By this point, Fiona was also capturing the attention of fellow artists. Kanye West was a huge fan.

"Fiona Apple, Sleep to Dream. One of my favourite opening lines to a song... 'I have never been so insulted in all my life!'" [46]

– Kanye West

Please note that Kanye is incorrect, as the line in question does not open the song. But it's the thought that counts!

Meanwhile, Macy Gray attempted to cover the song but found it too difficult.

"Her songs are so moody, and if you take it out of that, it doesn't sound right". [67]

– Macy Gray

A Stéphane Sednaoui-directed music video landed in May 1997, where Fiona sings around an apartment with allusions to insomnia. The video won the MTV Video Music Award for Best New Artist in a Video that same year. Fiona's speech is so noteworthy that we have granted it a separate section later in this chapter.

• Criminal

"Criminal" was the third and final official single from *Tidal*, arriving on September 16, 1997. Reportedly, Fiona wrote it in forty-five minutes during a lunch break between recordings just to prove she could easily pen a hit. As it turns out, she totally could! This song proved to be Fiona's biggest number yet, reaching #9 on the Canada Rock/Alternative chart, #4 on the US Alternative Airplay, and #2 on the US Adult Alternative Songs. Peaking at #21 on the Billboard Hot 100, it remains her only entry on that list.

"[It's about] feeling bad for getting something so easily by using your sexuality." [46]

– Fiona Apple

With 1,000,000 copies sold, "Criminal" has been certified platinum in the US. Everyone loved it, from Rolling Stone calling it the 423rd Best Song of All Time (2021 list) and VH1 placing it as the 71st Greatest Song of the 90s. The Grammys took note, their 40th award show nominating it for Best Rock Song and Best Female Rock Vocal Performance, the latter of which she won! When asked where her Grammy was, she replied:

"I don't know where it is right now. I gave it away." [69]

– Fiona Apple

In later years, she managed to remember a few details about its whereabouts. In true Fiona fashion, she had attempted to use it for a good cause.

"For the longest time it was at somebody's house and they wouldn't give it back to

me, and I said I was going to give it to my
grandmother, but I was really going to
donate it to a school so they could auction it
off. But it turns out you can't auction it off.
So now it's in this office in this school, and I
haven't gotten around to writing them to
get it back." [70]

– Fiona Apple

The music video for "Criminal" proved incredibly conse-
quential for Fiona's career, and as a result, it warrants its own
section later. Regardless, one could easily assume that this is
most casual fans' first Fiona song they'll think of. Even Jennifer
Lopez pole-danced to the song in *Hustlers*.

"Listen, I just want to say: I would give my
song to Jennifer Lopez to dance to for free,
any day, any time." [71]

– Fiona Apple

And from this point onward, without much warning, Fiona
Apple was a superstar, whether she liked it or not.

"I was seventeen, and everything from
seventeen to twenty was in the public eye.
That was a very confused time just because

of my age and it was also a very confused time just because of everything that I was going through with all this stuff [...] I've felt so much that I'm so so lucky that this happened so fast for me. Because you think about those bands that play for nine years in some club, you know, in nowhere land waiting for some ANR guy to come and recognise them and exploit them. But I never had to do that, so I felt I was here and I didn't have to pay my dues. But you fucking realise that you're gonna have to pay your dues somehow, and I ended up paying my dues by having to get used to it all in public. So me getting used to it was my first impression. My confusion was the first impression. My contradictions were the first impressions. And I suppose there's a part of me right now that kind of wants to go out and do it again just to erase everything that happened before." [72]

– Fiona Apple

Other Noteworthy Songs

Several tracks on *Tidal* deserve additional discussion, but none were as fervently reported on as "Sullen Girl". The dominoes fell when an Italian journalist asked her about the lyrics, in particular:

"They don't know I used to sail the deep and tranquil sea, but he washed me 'shore and he took my pearl and left an empty shell of me." [71]

– "Sullen Girl" lyrics

Never one to mince her words, Fiona detailed her rape story, which had inspired this song.

"When I was 12, I was raped by a stranger, and that's what this song is basically about because I felt like everybody in my life thought there was something wrong with me, and it was just me wondering, 'was that what changed me?' [...] It was really just because I felt like 'well, I used to be this really lighthearted person. And I am a lighthearted person, but everyone looks at me, and they think I'm really serious and

depressed and sullen. Do I come off that way because of this experience?" It was something that caused me a lot of pain, and I just felt like, 'Is that why I'm being misunderstood?' So that's when it started getting bad when people started assuming that things were bad and started labelling me as a sick person." [73]

– Fiona Apple

Once this information became public, interviewers were insensitive to her traumas and repeatedly referenced the incident in their questions. Ever the fighting person, Fiona took these conversations in her stride.

"You want to ask about when I was raped? Please don't act like I have got food in my teeth. It's out in the open. It's not something that I'm embarrassed about, so don't act like it's something that I should be embarrassed about." [20]

– Fiona Apple

"The First Taste" and "Never Is a Promise" were released as promotional singles.

"The First Taste" has a music video where Fiona dances in a room full of people and sings the words on her floor. Even diehard fans are often unaware about this clip's existence, perhaps because the scene is considered by viewers to be "cringy", "campy", and "very 90s".

The confessional "Never Is a Promise" is not only notable as part of her original demos that got her signed but also due to Van Dyke Parks' backing string arrangement. He is best known for his work with Brian Wilson and the Beach Boys. Yet despite the song's constant love from fans, Fiona no longer has any interest in performing it live.

"I don't want to sing that because I don't want to be back in that place." [74]

– Fiona Apple

Oh well, at least we'll always have the music video, where Fiona sings on a nighttime street as a slight wind disrupts her hair.

As for "Pale September", it's fascinating to hear her sister, Maude Maggart, providing backing vocals on a song that relates to herself.

"That's about a guy who went out with my sister's best friend, and he lost his virginity in my bed with her. Then I went out with him." [46]

– Fiona Apple

With these songs neatly tucked away, everyone could be proud of what they achieved, Fiona most of all.

"When I made my first record, I really did think that that was gonna solve everything. I thought that this will be my 'hello, this is me, nice to meet you, let's skip it all and if you like this then let's be best friends forever and I'll always be loyal and let's hug." [75]

– Fiona Apple

But what nobody knew was that such an unignorable collection would have consequences and the genuine tidal wave was only just roaring over the horizon.

"I remember when I was making the album, I used to ride my bike down the beach, and there's always these skateboarder kids around my age on the bike path, all doing their tricks and stuff. And I would ride by, and no one knew who I was or anything like that. I remember thinking, 'In a few months, I'm gonna be able to pass, and I'll feel really good about myself there because they're gonna think that I'm cool because I'm gonna feel like they know who I am.' [But now] I've had people come and stand

right next to me and they don't even say it to me but say something, like, 'Fiona Apple's really stupid' [...] They think that it's a cool thing to do. Go say something mean to the famous girl because she's famous, she's evil or something like that. So now I'm intimidated more so, except it's for a different thing." [76]

– Fiona Apple

4.2.
Andy Slater
and Jon Brion

"You do have to take a deep breath every so often, but I would worry more if I thought it was just an act because I think people would eventually catch on to that. But Fiona speaks from the heart." [18]

– Andy Slater, Manager/Producer

Andy Slater can take credit as the guy who discovered Fiona and the mastermind behind the *Tidal* production. Yet despite his belief in her, Fiona's trauma did not allow her to trust any older men at this time, and she would refuse to sit next to him.

However, if one man earned Fiona's confidence and respect during the *Tidal* session, it would be Jon Brion. Brion's credentials extend far out into the music landscape, from soundtracks (2004's *Eternal Sunshine of the Spotless Mind*, 2015's *Trainwreck*, 2017's *Lady Bird*) to big name album production (Frank Ocean's *Blonde*, Beyonce's *Lemonade*, Kanye West's *Late Registration*). The man is forever sought after and very busy.

But one could argue that it was back on *Tidal* that Brion's career flourished simultaneously with Fiona's. He performed vibraphone on most of the album as well as other assorted instruments, but more importantly, the pair would work together on many future projects as we shall soon see.

"She's aware of the cause and effect of things, but she's not calculating in the sense that a lot of people in pop music are. She's got no problem biting the hand that feeds her if she thinks the hand is up to no good." [43]

– Jon Brion, Producer

4.3.
Relationship
Status: Tyson

"It's very closed-minded and very naive. A lot of people who are saying that I just don't know today's world. They probably didn't have their first relationship until they were 18. I had mine at 14. I had parents who were splitting up all the time. I know a lot about relationships. I've been in therapy my whole life. And it's the same with a lot of kids today. It's not that I've just got an active imagination. These songs are my story." [18]

– Fiona Apple

Fiona's first kiss was in ninth grade with a boy named Eddie, who inspired songs like "Shadowboxer" and "Criminal". However, most of *Tidal* focuses on a boy later revealed to be named Tyson. The two met when he was rollerblading around the Columbia University campus.

"After that day, we hung out with each other for ten days straight without going home." [20]

– Tyson, Ex Boyfriend

They dated for two and a half years, with Fiona admitting she lost her virginity to him. However, when he expressed interest in another girl, Fiona cut him off.

"I remember it being all my fault. Well, 95% my fault. I started seeing this other girl and liking her a little bit. And [Fiona] said one day, 'I never want to see you again.' And then a year later an album's out." [20]

– Tyson, Ex Boyfriend

Of course, Fiona found catharsis in her writing, with songs like "Never is a Promise" and "Sleep to Dream" ringing especially loudly.

"'Sleep to Dream' pretty much it felt like that's what she was saying to me the last time I talked to her. And the video was set up in a way so it looks like her bedroom [...] [I saw Fiona] kneeling on the ground, looking through the TV, looking straight at me." [20]

– Tyson, Ex Boyfriend

Fiona has since stated she does not hate Tyson anymore.

"I've been called by boyfriends that I'm not even a girl. I'm a creature. More than once." [77]

– Fiona Apple

4.4.
Age is Just a Number

"You are too young to be reading Maya Angelou books. Do that when you're, like, 50 and you've got no life. You think you're depressed now? Wait until you get to my age." [18]

– Howard Stern

"I hate it when people ask 'how you can talk about such adult themes? How you can possibly know so much so young?'" [18]

– Fiona Apple

"Some guy in Europe actually told me that he thought that I had made up everything that I had written about. He didn't think that I could have experienced that much being 19. And it just makes feel like, damn, there's a big generation gap." [78]

– Fiona Apple

"You know, the age thing really bugs me. Do people have more of a right to not like what I say because I'm nineteen? I'm up here because of what I write. Obviously, I must know something, or I wouldn't have been nominated for Best New Artist. Sometimes it's like, 'You're right. My mother wrote these songs." [23]

– Fiona Apple

Perhaps the most impressive aspect surrounding Fiona's sudden shot up the fame ladder was that she was only 18 when Tidal was released. For this reason, many people struggled to believe that such old-soul words could come from an age usually lacking life experience. Even producer Andy Slater had his doubts.

"I was not entirely convinced that this person sitting in front of me—who was clearly seventeen—had written those words. At first, I thought it was a Milli Vanilli thing." [79]

– Andy Slater, Manager/Producer

"It sounded like a 30-year-old singer who had written a lifetime's worth of material. I thought someone was playing a joke on me." [61]

– Andy Slater, Manager/Producer

"I don't know how I would feel, old or young. I don't understand how people can really answer questions like that. I have no basis of comparison. I've never been anyone else." [80]

– Fiona Apple

Fiona hadn't even played on stage when she was signed; hence she was forced to learn the ropes quickly. Which she did, in the most Fiona ways possible: with her vulnerability on her sleeves beneath raised fists.

"I think everybody's got a different life experience. You could get me and 10 other 19 year olds and we'll all be different people. We've all had different 19 years. So, no, I'm not wise beyond my 19 years. Maybe somebody else's 19 years, perhaps, but not mine." [60]

– Fiona Apple

"I'm such an incredibly stupidly sensitive person that everything that happens to me, I experience it really intensely. I feel everything very deeply. And when you feel things deeply and you think about things a lot and you think about how you feel, you learn a lot about yourself. And when you know yourself, you know life." [81]

– Fiona Apple

"The whole reason why I wanted to make an album in the first place is because I was so tired of trying to explain my personality to people. I was so uncomfortable with the social situations that I thought, I really,

really thought that if I had a CD of songs that I could just put that out in the world and then everyone would understand me, and then I would have all the friends in the world. And I think most people find out that what they thought, if they got rich or if they got famous, that everything was going to be solved and it wasn't. But in my case, not only did I not get what I wanted, I got exactly the opposite of what I wanted to have happen. Instead of having everybody be my friend and understand me, everybody thought I was awful." [82]

– Fiona Apple

4.5.
That Criminal
Video

"There's no way for me to have a clearer perspective on this because this is basically just five minutes of somebody making me look really pretty. How am I supposed to have any kind of problem with that unless somebody else presents a problem to me? Which is the whole point of it. I'm treating the audience that is watching this video the same way that the character in this song treats the man. 'Look at me, look how pretty I am. I don't have to give you anything else because look how pretty I am. Look how successful I can be. And look how much power I can get just by letting this light shine on me in this certain way.*"* [83]

– Fiona Apple

Wherever Fiona Apple was before, the music video for "Criminal" exploded her name like a sonic boom across the planet, and not for the best of reasons. Labelled terms such as "heroin chic" and "jailbait", viewers were either turned on or horrified by a skinny doped-up looking Fiona rolling around dark rooms wearing nothing but a tank top and panties. All the while, other half-naked bodies were strewn across the highly voyeuristic, sexually charged scene.

"I called Mark, and we talked about his idea that the song is about guilty pleasures and sexual deviance—me being in this house full of people, going around and experimenting, feeling a little bad about it, but enjoying it all the same. It corresponded with my meaning of the song. Making the video was a huge step for me, personally, because I'm not comfortable doing any of that. When we were shooting, there were all these female extras who are paid to be pretty. They tried to make me pretty, but that's not what I do:

I am paid to sing and perform. So I'm there, as insecure as ever, surrounded by all these dancer models strutting around in bikinis. I had a stand-in, and she was gorgeous. I was dying. I've gone through stages where I hate my body so much that I won't even wear shorts and a bra in my house because if I pass a mirror, that's the end of my day.

So, it was a personal mission to do that video. To get up in front of all those gorgeous girls and strut my stuff. To convince myself, 'You've got something else going on here'. It was a huge step. But in the end, the truth is it's fun to be up there and know that you're in your underwear. Even though I know I'm exploiting my sexuality in a certain way, it's fun! It boosts my ego. Which is exactly what the song is about." [23]

– Fiona Apple

The clip was directed by Mark Romanek, whose long list of videos includes "Closer" by Nine Inch Nails, "Can't Stop" by Red Hot Chili Peppers, "Shake It Off" by Taylor Swift, and "Scream" by Michael and Janet Jackson (which was listed as the most expensive music video ever made by the Guinness World Records).

> *"It's nothing against Mark, and it was nothing against the art of the video, [but] I got so much shit for it. And, you know, all the people that are there during the video telling you how great it is, they're not there anymore. So then you have all these people that are there going, 'You sell out! You slut!'"* [84]

– Fiona Apple

Fiona has since distanced herself from the video and has been less eager to follow other people's video visions as her career has progressed.

> *"The shit that got me popular was the stuff that I was not proud of. It makes me feel really stupid. I wanted to be like every other girl you see in videos, and that's why it's embarrassing. But the way that I justified [the treatment] is that the song is about someone talking to God about a mistake they've been making. And so I actually did think for a while that the video made sense. But I think*

the thing that screwed it up is how fuckin'
horrified I look. I really look like I'm doing
something wrong, instead of playing it with a
little bit of a wink. I just couldn't do it. "[43]

– Fiona Apple

Apple later donated a year's worth of Criminal profits to immigrant criminal-defence cases.

"I haven't watched the video in a while. I'm
still in touch with Mark Romanek, and he's a
great guy and he's my friend. That was just a
situation where everything was set up when
I got there. I didn't have the treatment of
how the video was supposed to be. They were
expecting somebody to come up and be like,
'Yeah! I'm sexy! I'm stripping!' versus somebody
being like, 'I'm sad. "'[43]

– Fiona Apple

"I didn't look like myself. It's kind of ruined the song for me. No offence to Mark Romanek. Well, I guess offence. I have total qualms about it now."[85]

– Fiona Apple

4.6.
That MTV
Award Speech

*"I was cast in the crazy role,
and I was perfect for it."*[86]

– Fiona Apple

If you thought the video for "Criminal" was the last of young Fiona's controversial troubles, you haven't heard anything yet. After winning the 1997 MTV Video Music Award for Best New Artist in a Video for "Sleep to Dream" (beating Hanson, the bookie favourites), Fiona took to the stage to unleash the following unorthodox speech:

*"I didn't prepare a speech, and I'm sorry, but
I'm glad that I didn't because I'm not going
to do this like everybody else does. You see,*

Maya Angelou said that we as human beings at our best can only create opportunities and I'm going to use this opportunity the way that I wanna use it. So what I wanna say is, everybody out there that's watching, everybody that's watching this world, this world is bullshit, and you shouldn't model your life—wait a second!—you shouldn't model your life about what you think we think is cool and what we're wearing and what we're saying and everything. Go with yourself. And it's just stupid that I'm in this world, but you're all very cool to me."

– Fiona Apple,
1997 MTV Video Music Award Speech

The amount of content that spewed from this incident could fill its own book. While the initial audience appeared to cheer Fiona's fresh stance, the consensus that followed was less kind, with people seeing Fiona as a bratty child. Fiona has spoken on the topic many times with varying degrees of heat.

"When I walked backstage, I was proud of myself—and they gave me the silent treatment! They pretended I wasn't there! [That was] the moment I learned that they needed me more than I need them. [It was] one of the best things I've ever done."[18]

– Fiona Apple

"I was there thinking, 'I'm in high school. I'm in a cafeteria. I have to walk by people that are going to laugh at me.' Instead of just walking by and feeling like I've been intimidated like that a million times, I didn't want that to be who I was. This cool feeling of wanting to take responsibility and make decisions for myself and not feel like I had to hide my emotions—that was a great thing. Now, I don't have the feeling like I'm the kind of person who never speaks out. Now I don't have that itch anymore."[43]

– Fiona Apple

"When I won, I felt like a sellout. I felt that I deserved recognition, but the recognition I was getting was for the wrong reasons. I felt that now in the blink of an eye, all of those people who didn't give a shit who I was or what I thought were now all at once just humouring, appeasing me. And not because of my talent. But instead because of the fact that, somehow, with the help of my record company and my makeup artist, my stylist, and my press, I had successfully created the illusion that I was perfect and pretty and rich and, therefore, living a higher quality of life. I had saved myself from misfit status, but I'd betrayed my own kind by becoming a paper doll in order to be accepted."[20]

– Fiona Apple

"I went from being 'tragic waif ethereal victim' to being 'brat bitch loose cannon'. I just had something in my mind, and I just said it, and that's really the foreshadowing of my entire career and my entire life. When I have something to say, I'll say it."[20]

– Fiona Apple

"*My whole life, people have been saying, 'Why are you so angry?' and I didn't know what the hell they were talking about. After I saw myself at the MTV Awards, I realised, wow, I do kind of come off a bit intense. I wasn't upset at MTV at all. I didn't mean to come off that way. But I think it's good if I appeared a bit angry. People are too complacent [...] I think I did a wonderful thing. I have absolutely no regrets. I've gotten a lot of shit for the things I said when I got my award. Some people say I made an ass out of myself. But I had an opportunity, and I took it the way I wanted to. The people I was talking to understood what I was saying.*" [23]

– Fiona Apple

"*I was so miserable back then that I pretty much blocked out everything that happened. I know that I was real pouty. And I know that I was also being yanked around everywhere and that I had good reason to be pouty. But I just know that I was so miserable.*" [87]

– Fiona Apple

"I never said the world was bullshit, I just said **this** world was bullshit, referring to the room that I was in and the whole music scene. It's not bullshit anymore. It's the bull who ate that shit and then shit it out again, and then ate that shit and then shit it out again, and then ate that shit and then shit it out again, and then ate that shit and then shit it out again, and now it's **that** bullshit."[88]

– Fiona Apple

"That [speech] was a huge moment in my life that I will never, ever regret, and that I have never regretted, no matter how embarrassed I might have been by it at a certain point. I knew it was one of those moments where you have to be a really good parent to yourself and go: 'This is a time you can get out there and just say it, you have to because if you don't do it now you set a precedent for yourself at these things. You shut up your entire life at school, you took all this shit and you were quiet, look how it made you feel. You're at this thing right now, this magnified high school class and now you got a chance to go up and say something? Don't be shy. No matter how it comes out, just let it come out.' So I'm really glad that I did that and I think that that set me on a good path."[89]

– Fiona Apple

4.7.
That General Backlash

"I say the right thing, but I look the wrong way, so they say something about the way I look. I look the right way, but I say the wrong thing, so they say something mean about what I said. I have a temper. I have lots of rage inside. I have lots of sadness inside of me. And I really, really, really can't stand assholes. If I'm in front of one, and I happen to be in a public place, and I lose my shit—and that's a possibility—that's not going to be any good to me, but I won't be able to help it, because I'll want to defend myself."[1]

– Fiona Apple

As Fiona was finding herself in this confusing world of stardom, the world itself seemed equally confused by her. This led to many misconceptions about who she really was.

"It all kind of gets blown out of proportion. You say one thing once and then it gets mentioned in everything, so it sounds like you're saying it all the time. But I don't think I was any more miserable than anybody else, so I don't know. I've never been anybody else so I don't know. I wasn't that happy."[90]

– Fiona Apple

"For a long time when I was younger, I felt I needed to hide who I was, because I felt it was not accepted to be a sensitive person. People misinterpreted who I was, basically, because of my appearance. If you are not engaged in conversations and you are just thinking by yourself, you just happened to not be smiling, in my surroundings, I was perceived to be depressed, sullen, and sad. I hated the fact that people thought that of me. They wouldn't believe that I wasn't that way."[91]

– Fiona Apple

"That's a big misconception about me. I'm not shy. I don't speak if I don't have anything to say. That's what tact is. Tact is the art of saying nothing when there's nothing to say."[92]

– Fiona Apple

Sadly, public backlash snowballed and ranged from genuine concern to cruel jokes. Perhaps the ugliest came from comedian Janeane Garofalo, who recorded a spoken-word parody track mocking Fiona's MTV speech, titled "A Reading From the Book of Apple". Here is an excerpt:

"You shouldn't model your life about what you think that we think is cool. Even though I have an eating disorder and I have somehow sold out to the patriarchy in this culture that says that lean is better. Even though I have done that, and have done a video wherein I wear underwear so that you young girls out there can covet, and feel bad about what you have, and how thin you're not. The point is, I have done it, I am lean. That's why I did succeed sooner than maybe other musicians that maybe were better songwriters, better lyricists, better vocalists... I can't say that.

But I do know this: This world is bullshit. Did I say this world is bullshit? 'Cause it is. And my boyfriend can make you disappear. "[93]

– Janeane Garofalo, "Comedian"

Fiona responded in the most Fiona way possible, by penning a poem which ended with the following four lines:

"Well, I best be off now to primp and preen,
But before I go, here's an end to your mean,
I be a paradox of gestures and genes,
But you are a cowardly bitch, Janeane. "[94]

– Fiona Apple

Of course, Fiona's fighting exterior was a soft shell around a vulnerable tissue beneath.

"Since that video was made, I've gained about 20 pounds on purpose so that people can see me like that. I know what I'm doing. Bitch. I'm going to get bigger and bigger, and the girls are going to see that I don't care and that I feel better like that. Of course I have an eating disorder. Every girl in fucking America has an eating disorder. Janeane Garofalo has an eating disorder, and that's why she's upset. Every girl has an eating disorder because of videos like that. But that's exactly what the video is about. When I say, 'I've been a bad, bad girl, I've been careless with a delicate man' – well, in a way I've been careless with a delicate audience, and I've gotten success that way, and I've lived in my ego that way, and I feel bad about it. And that's what the song's about, and therefore, that's what the video looks like."[20]

– Fiona Apple

To be fair to Janeane Garofalo, let's give her a chance to reevaluate her decisions.

"All I can say is, yep, I did it. I have to take full responsibility. In the end I'm not pleased that a young woman's feelings were hurt by it. It was one of those deals where you don't think about it. That's just me being a dick [...] In 13 years of doing stand-up, I have discovered time and again, people get hurt a lot when you think you're just doing comedy."[20]

– Janeane Garofalo, "Comedian"

And to be fair to Fiona, let's give her the rest of the chapter to explain why she has this moody reputation in the first place.

"I think I get this reputation because I write all these songs that are very angry towards people. And it's all about trying to seem like I've got it all under control. It's not true. I never feel like that when I'm writing the songs. They're all kind of pep talks and so kind of coming true later on, like, after like a year or two, I'll finally actually feel as strong as I did when I tried to pretend that I was that strong."[36]

– Fiona Apple

"I only write when I'm angry or sad or something because that's when I just have to write. And I only will work if I absolutely have to. And if I'm having a good time and I'm happy and things were going really well, why would I want to stop what I'm doing to going write at the piano?"[95]

– Fiona Apple

"On many of the songs I am actually saying those things to particular people in such a way that, even if they don't realise it's them, they'll feel uncomfortable. I'm not religious, but I think I've been treated unfairly a lot and I want justice to be done every time. I'm not saying, 'You have sinned and you're going to hell'. It's, 'You're going to the hell of being exiled from me."[11]

– Fiona Apple

"I'm really, really sensitive, and it's not easy. I'm a person who does not have a thick skin. And I don't think I really want a thick skin. I don't want to grow a callus all over myself. I don't feel like I would be able to make anything that I would love if I did that."[45]

– Fiona Apple

4.8.
Beauty is Only Skin Deep

As we've already seen, a lot of positive and negative attention that falls upon Fiona has to do with her looks. People either concentrate on her pretty face or her skinny frame, ignoring the songwriter completely. But such things are of little importance to our heroine.

"I'm going to help some little girl out there. I'm going to let her know that I have stretch marks on my ass, and bunions, that I don't have my shit together. Please say that I don't have my shit together at all. I want to give that girl some hope."[96]

– Fiona Apple

"I'm not like a fashion horse [...] the funniest fucking home video of me ever is when I'm, like, five years old and it lasts about ten minutes. [...] I'm making this costume which I was always doing, like, with custom construction paper and tape. The whole time my sister's dancing around just enjoying the music. The whole time I'm, like, 'I'm not ready! I'm not ready yet! I'm not ready yet!' because I just keep on taping these things [...] I finally finish it, take one spin, and fall flat on my face."[97]

– Fiona Apple

"I got a perm when I was ten with teeth missing. I remember going into school and they called me lion that day instead of dog. It's my only attempt at ever trying to like do something other than that."[98]

– Fiona Apple

"[Weight] is a sensitive subject because it's not something that should be talked about. There is nothing wrong with me. I'm healthy and I shouldn't even have to say any of that. What makes me unhealthy and puts me in danger is that kind of scrutiny itself. It's the same as being bullied at school, and just because you're getting older, it doesn't mean that you aren't hurt by it. You could make anybody cry if you told them that they're ugly. I don't even know what I'm being accused of. Do they think I'm on drugs? That I have a life-threatening illness? Do they think that I'm anorexic? At this point, emotionally, it doesn't get easier to hear those criticisms—but it gets easier to be resolute about my reaction to it. Which is just: Go ahead and call me ugly, call me skinny, call me crazy and speculate as much as you want, but not at a show."[99]

– Fiona Apple

"I don't think I'll ever have an idea of what I look like to the rest of the world. It's all your own perception. I could easily be concerned with how I'm taken and then have all the good stuff filtered through to me and choose to believe that. For the rest of my life it'd be the truth for me, but not the whole truth."[100]

– Fiona Apple

4.9.
Relationship Status: David Blaine

"David and I are both completely fucked-up. We're the most fucked-up people I know."[24]

– Fiona Apple

In perhaps one of the weirder romantic matchups, Fiona and illusionist-magician David Blaine started dating around the time *Tidal* landed. They met at a 1997 Grammys after-party, and Blaine used all of his pickup tricks. Literally. After showing her some card magic, the two agreed to go on a date, where Blaine showed off his levitating skills.

"He has an amazing lure. No matter how infatuated I've been with any guy, I always

want them to go away. And I don't really get it. The first time that he called, I said to my mom, 'You know how I never want to spend time with anybody? Well, if there's anyone who's going to pull me away from that, it's going to be this guy.' From the first time, I talked to him. He's just full of everything."[101]

– Fiona Apple

The couple lasted about a year but have remained on good terms. This is fortunate for David, who got Fiona's name permanently inked into his skin.

"He did it as a surprise. He had talked about it, but I kept telling him not to do it. I would feel stupid if somebody had to get me removed. It's not like he'll ever have to get it removed, though, because we'll always stay best friends."[80]

– Fiona Apple

This is not entirely true. In later years, Apple expressed her disgust that David was listed in Jeffrey Epstein's black book.

4.10.
Relationship Status: Marilyn Manson

"The funniest sound I've heard in the past year is when Mom yelled, 'Sweetie, Marilyn Manson's on the phone!'"[46]

– Fiona Apple

"There's Fiona, my candle-burning vampire child, who stays up all night long and gets phone messages from Marilyn Manson."[24]

– Diane McAfee, Fiona's Mom

No, Marilyn Manson and Fiona Apple were never an official item. But there was a period where it looked possible, starting with Manson's 1997 song, "Apple of Sodom". Released as part of David Lynch's *Lost Highway* soundtrack, the song was semi-inspired by Manson's feelings for Fiona.

"I met Fiona Apple at the Grammy Awards after-party the other night. She's this little singer who no one's heard of. I'm a huge fan of her music."[102]

– Marilyn Manson

The two attended the premiere of Howard Stern's *Private Parts* together.

"Oh, it's just an act, I like to act angry. Me and Manson got together; he said, 'I'm going to act like a Satanist, and you act like a brat, and everyone will pay attention to us, and then we'll both say we're misunderstood, and then we'll run off the edge of the earth."[20]

– Fiona Apple

The ever-articulate gentleman Manson concluded why their relationship would never work with the following:

"She's so sexy and fragile, definitely too fragile for me. If I was ever to be put in a circumstance where I could have sex with her, I would decline because her vagina is probably too precious to be dirtied by my filthy cock."[102]

– Marilyn Manson

It seemed like sweet Fiona had a knack for attracting disastrous rockstars. Another example came with Jane's Addiction guitarist, Dave Navarro. When the two were on the same lineup for the KROQ Almost Acoustic Christmas show in LA, Navarro left a message on her dressing room wall which read *"Dear Fiona, have fun. Love, D.N."* It was written in his blood.

"In my deranged head, I viewed it as sending her a message with the blood that pumps through my heart to her. It was my life blood that I was symbolically sharing. I thought we would relate on multiple levels, because we're both passionate musicians and artists. In my head, it was a grand, romantic statement that she would find very touching."[103]

– Dave Navarro

There is no official statement about Fiona following up on the gesture, but the word on the street is that she did not.

4.11.
Fiona Apple:
MTV Unplugged

A lright, now that we've got the sidelines stuff out of the way, let's get back to the music! Starting with Fiona Apple's very own MTV Unplugged session, on July 29, 1997. Here she performed "Shadowboxer", "Sleep To Dream", "Criminal", and a Jimi Hendrix cover of "Angel".

"That thing is weird to do. Because there's a couple of times where you have to stop because you did a wrong note or something like that. Whereas in a normal show, the audience is going on at a natural pace. With the [Unplugged] show you have to stop when

something technical was wrong and the audience just sits there and stares at you. "[104]

– Fiona Apple

4.12.
Pleasantville
Songs

Around the 1998 *Tidal* era, Fiona covered some songs for the fantasy comedy-drama film, *Pleasantville*. These were Percy Mayfield's "Please Send Me Someone to Love" and a superb version of the Beatles' "Across the Universe". The latter received a music video where Fiona wears headphones as she sings the lyrics, seemingly oblivious to the destruction of the *Pleasantville* set behind her. It was directed by Paul Thomas Anderson, which proved to be yet another monumental meeting in Fiona's life, as we'll see shortly.

"I had Beatles all over my room. On my doorknob, it said Enter Beatlemania and on the way out it said Exit Beatlemania. I had a huge 'Let It Be' poster with the four of them

next to my bed. And after a while, when I did make friends, I made friends that loved Beatles. That was our thing. And we each had our people. I was John Lennon [...] I didn't have a crush on him; I just thought he was God. "[105]

– Fiona Apple

On a weird side note that nobody knows, it was also during this phase that Fiona was offered the lead in the fourth Karate Kid movie.

"It would have been a disaster. "[20]

– Fiona Apple

4.13.
Tidal Tour

"That's the thing about how everything happened so fast for me. It's a big break on one hand. But, then again, it's a big kick in the ass because I had to develop my stage presence in front of everybody."[106]

– Fiona Apple

Talk about hitting the ground running; Fiona slammed into the gig circuit at a million miles an hour. Some of the then-18-year-old's first performances were on *Saturday Night Live* and the *Tonight Show*.

"I wasn't that nervous. It's hard to be when you don't know what you're actually nervous

about. I had no idea what it was going to be like. "[49]

– Fiona Apple

"I was so obsessive in my own little world of things that I don't know what the hell I was thinking about the audience. I still pretend that they're not there because I feel like that's the best thing to do for them. I think that ignoring them is the best is my part in our relationship [...] I was probably just thinking I have to get out of here and go to a hotel and try to open every door in the hallway which is something that I used to have to do [as an OCD thing]. "[107]

– Fiona Apple

Fiona embarked on a tour from late 1996 to 1998 to support her debut, playing across The States with some European dates in the UK, France, Germany, and Sweden.

"This whole music thing is 80% a personal mission and 20% a career. It was a mission to prove that I had something to offer. There is no way three years ago I could have gotten up on stage [...] It's a whole new experience for me to be able to be proud of myself and to stand up to the scrutiny of anybody, the press, the audiences. It wasn't that long ago that I couldn't even stand up to the scrutiny of my high school."[18]

– Fiona Apple

Unfortunately, she cancelled her final 21 slots because of "personal family problems." No further details were given, but there has been some speculation that this was an excuse for greater mental health concerns. Such rumours were additionally fuelled by the infamous comment she gave Spin in 2019:

"I'm going to die young. I'm going to cut another album, and I'm going to do good things, help people, and then I'm going to die."[24]

– Fiona Apple

Part Five
When the Pawn

5.1.
Album: When the Pawn (1999)

FULL TITLE:

When the pawn hits the conflicts he thinks like a king/ What he knows throws the blows when he goes to the fight/ And he'll win the whole thing 'fore he enters the ring/ There's no body to batter when your mind is your might/ So when you go solo, you hold your own hand/ And remember that depth is the greatest of heights/ And if you know where you stand, then you know where to land/ And if you fall it won't matter, cuz you'll know that you're right.

1. On the Bound (5:22)
2. To Your Love (3:40)
3. Limp (3:29)
(second single)
4. Love Ridden (3:22)
5. Paper Bag (3:39)
(third single)
6. A Mistake (4:56)
7. Fast as You Can (4:38)
(first single)
8. The Way Things Are (4:16)
9. Get Gone (4:07)
10. I Know (4:55)

TOTAL RUNTIME: 42:39

"I told people for a while that I wasn't sure I was even gonna have a second album. I was real afraid that I wasn't gonna be able to write like on the road because I have weird rituals and everything. I can't write if

anyone else is within an 80-mile surrounding. But I've been writing a lot. It's all in my head, though, because I can't play piano on the road. So I'm really frustrated because I just want to be able to, like, make it actually a tangible thing. To be able to like to hear it and play it and stuff and it's all here now. So it's kind of driving me crazy." [108]

– Fiona Apple

Fiona recorded her sophomore work across many Californian studios (Andora Studio, Chateau Brion Studio, NRG Recording Studios, Ocean Way Studio, One On One South, Presence Studios, Woodwinds). It was released by Epic/Clean Slate on November 9, 1999.

"I think that you'll find that there's a lot more blaming myself on the first album. On this one, there's a lot more confidence. There's a lot more decision-making. Something that is very important to me about this album is that I was so anxious to make it because the last album, I let a lot of the decisions be made for me as to how to do it in everything. On this album, I knew that

I was going to be able to choose everyone that I was working with and to do it my own way and doing my own hours. There's a lot more of a clear view on things in this album. And also a lot more of a sense of humour." [109]

– Fiona Apple

"I write pretty well, I'm a good singer, and I can play my songs well enough on piano. You're good at everything else." [110]

– Fiona Apple (said to Jon Brion)

As you may remember, Jon Brion's skills covered much of *Tidal*, and his contributions must have impressed Fiona as she swiftly hired the man for *When the Pawn* too. Except, this time, he was promoted right up to the producer rank.

"Fiona is deeply incredible. Just really, really good. It was a pleasure every day to work on the material. She is a total dream to work with. She is the easiest, nicest, most considerate, most forthright person I have ever worked with in a production capacity.

No one even comes close. " [111]

– Jon Brion, Producer

Other familiar *When the Pawn* musicians included Patrick Warren (playing keyboards) and, more importantly, Matt Chamberlain taking on percussion/drummer duties again. A guy named Mike Elizondo took the bass—remember him for later. Meanwhile, Jim Keltner took on extra drum duties, a man whose sticks can be heard on recordings as far back as George Harrison, John Lennon, and the Beach Boys, but as recent as Phoebe Bridgers, John Mayar, and Lana Del Rey. No wonder he has been labelled "the leading session drummer in America."

"The way I work is this: I figure my songs out; every song I could go sit down and play at the piano, and it would be a skeleton of what's actually on the album. I'm always set on rhythm and structure, words and melodies, and I have an idea of all the different sounds that I want. But so many things that mean so much to me and that are such a big part of my pride in the album are completely created from, mainly, John and Matt. But John doesn't change structure or ask me to do things. I don't want the world

to think I don't come up with the structure of my songs. I want to say how much work John and Matt did; I even wanted to give them writing credit. But I also want to make it clear I'm not just walking in with two chords and my words, and they're finishing everything." [112]

– Fiona Apple

There was a lot to unpack on this record, but, initially, everyone only had one question... what's up with that title??

Title

"It came from being made fun of. And then, of course, it becomes a thing I'm being made fun of for." [113]

– Fiona Apple

Again, here is the full title:

When the pawn hits the conflicts he thinks like a king/ What he knows throws the blows when he goes to the fight/ And he'll win the whole thing 'fore he enters the ring/ There's no body to batter when your mind is your might/ So when you go solo, you hold your own hand/ And remember that depth is the greatest of heights/ And if you know where you stand, then you know where to land/ And if you fall it won't matter, cuz you'll know that you're right.

This 90-word poem was inspired by a Spin article that portrayed Fiona in a very negative light.

"They screwed me from the beginning. They knew what they were going to do with the story, and it didn't really matter what I said, but I said some things that they could very easily edit together and make me look like a moron. I was upset about it but thought, well, that's just what they do to you." [85]

– Fiona Apple

Things got worse. A subsequent Spin issue fell on Fiona's lap, in which readers had written to the publication, offering their unfavourable opinions of our protagonist based on that article.

"A month later, I was just going back on the road for another two-month run, and I was really tired. And I had just sat on the bus and there's Spin with Bjork on the cover and I picked it up and there were all these *terrible letters in reaction to my story. 'She's the most annoying thing in the world, etc.' And I got so upset, I was crying, and I didn't know how to make myself go on. Make myself feel like it was all going to be okay."* [85]

– Fiona Apple

Here is an example of one of those letters:

"Being a victim of rape is a trauma I would not wish on my worst enemy, but Fiona Apple's over-the-top melodrama and self-absorption make it difficult to feel any sort of sympathy for her. I am so tired of drama queens parading their woes under the public spotlight, as if victimhood was a trendy fashion statement. Fiona is an embarrassment to other survivors of sexual abuse." [114]

– SPIN Reader

Fiona immediately wrote this album's title, initially as some sort of a mantra to help her through the large-scale bullying.

"I sat down and wrote this poem in just a furious minute. It's not my best piece of writing or anything, but I was thinking that when it came time to record an album, it would be useful for me to remember this. It was another instance of writing something to help myself." [37]

– Fiona Apple

When released, it broke the Guinness World Record for the longest album title, with 444 characters.

"To anybody that has ever made fun of me for doing that, I say this: Are you in the Guinness Book of World Records? Thank you." [115]

– Fiona Apple

This feat has since been beaten by Chumbawamba, who has a title with 865 characters. For interest sake, that is here:

The Boy Bands Have Won, and All the Copyists and the Tribute Bands and the TV Talent Show Producers Have Won, If We Allow Our Culture to Be Shaped by Mimicry, Whether from

*Lack of Ideas or from Exaggerated Respect. You Should Never Try
to Freeze Culture. What You Can Do Is Recycle That Culture.
Take Your Older Brother's Hand-Me-Down Jacket and Re-Style
It, Re-Fashion It to the Point Where It Becomes Your Own. But
Don't Just Regurgitate Creative History, or Hold Art and Music
and Literature as Fixed, Untouchable and Kept Under Glass.
The People Who Try to 'Guard' Any Particular Form of Music
Are, Like the Copyists and Manufactured Bands, Doing It the
Worst Disservice, Because the Only Thing That You Can Do to
Music That Will Damage It Is Not Change It, Not Make It Your
Own. Because Then It Dies, Then It's Over, Then It's Done, and
the Boy Bands Have Won.*

"But now it totally looks like I was trying to
get publicity or say something to the world.
And I totally wasn't. I do things and they
just come off wrong. I wish I didn't have to
take shit for it, because it's not important
enough to me." [43]

– Fiona Apple

Sound

"I'm more confident this time. I can say what
I mean and not dramatise it too much. When

somebody sings in that over-the-top way, you can't hear what they're saying." [37]

– Fiona Apple

The album's sound diversified *Tidal*'s piano rock style by hitting harder into a more alternative realm, taking cues from art rock, art pop, jazz fusion, and chamber pop. Her lyrics remained around the vulnerability and empowerment of relationships (including those we have with ourselves), but it was undoubtedly a more mature affair, with Fiona finding stronger phrases to convey her messages.

"On the first record, there was some disparity between the Fiona that you talk to and Fiona the lyricist. With this record, there are more and more moments that sound like the person I hang out and talk with." [43]

– Jon Brion, Producer

"I think that I've gotten more to the point with how I state my feelings. I think that at the beginning I was so concerned with coming off like I was smart that I got really wordy." [116]

– Fiona Apple

Artwork

According to the credits, Fiona Apple came up with the cover art concept and design herself. Here we see her smiling broadly with a red hue, in contrast to her miserable reputation. Paul Thomas Anderson snapped it. Further art direction was accredited to Hooshik.

Over two decades later, in 2020, a vinyl reissue featured a much plainer cover where the shortened title sat upon a red background. According to Vinyl Me Please, Apple again chose this cover herself, which some have assumed has to do with distancing herself from Anderson, as we'll discuss in great detail as we continue.

Charts

Shipping 103,000 copies in its first week, *When the Pawn* hit 13 on the US Billboard 200. It has continued to steadily sell over the decades and was certified Platinum in 2020.

"I never worried about the whole second effort thing. I'm so proud of this record, and I think it's so much better than the last one." [117]

– Fiona Apple

Critical

Reviews for *When the Pawn* were positive, with almost every critic praising the album for being what *Tidal* was, except advancing that sound even further. Giving it full marks, Entertainment Weekly stated her music had "alluring dark circles under it" while "the melodies slither rather than pummel you". PopMatter went with an 80% score, saying, "She has defeated the odds to create a sophomore effort that is reflective of her earlier work but transcends those earlier limitations to create a new standard for pensive singer-songwriters in the new millennium." Meanwhile, Pitchfork praised that "her musical ideas and lyrics have caught up with the ability of her voice. The songs are well varied and transition smoothly from one to the other," awarding a very respectable 8/10. However, in a 2019 revaluation review, they pushed their score even higher, to a 9.4/10.

The record holds a 79 Metascore, which sadly illustrates that not everyone was happy. Perhaps the most vicious was NME, giving it a 5/10, complaining that "for her second album of Amos-aping MTV-branded Lilith Fair fodder, the barmiest, prettiest pretender to Tori's throne of corporate crackpot chic deals unashamedly in that tired and trusted heavyweight heart-tugging currency: relationships."

No matter! The critical acclaim only grew stronger as the years chugged on by. Slant Magazine called it the 79th-Best Album of the 90s. Rolling Stone ranked it as the 108th Greatest Album of All Time. It was nominated for Best Alternative Album at the Grammys but lost to Radiohead's *Kid A*.

Singles

• Fast As You Can

Released on October 5, 1999, "Fast as You Can" was the album's lead single.

"I wanted to explore different moods, the ups and downs of a relationship. When you get to the middle (of the song), that spell of confusion takes you out of the element for a minute, which is, of course, what happens emotionally. But the beat never changes." [37]

– Fiona Apple

The lyrical backstory kinda sucks. While on mushrooms at Johnny Depp's house, the actor led Fiona to a room where a mutual friend was waiting for her. Depp shut the door and left.

"Nothing bad happened, but I felt kind of used and uncomfortable with my friend making out with me. I used to just let things happen. I remember I wrote the bridge to 'Fast as You Can' in the car on the way home,

and he was playing Jimi Hendrix, and my mind was swirling things together." [1]

– Fiona Apple

With its unusual instrumentation and rhymes, many draw attention to Brior's production. But he is quick not to take credit.

"People hear certain things on the record and assume I came up with them. Like all the time changes in 'Fast As You Can.' All that stuff was there. All I did was to heighten pre-existing things. In terms of the colour changes, I am coordinating all of those, but the rhythms are absolutely Fiona's." [111]

– Fiona Apple

"Fast as You Can" was well received. The New York Times compared its keyboards to The Beatles' "Strawberry Fields Forever", while The Philadelphia Inquirer noted its "60s soul-jazz stomp." Newsweek and Spin described it as "galloping" and "skittery," respectively. The song hit #20 on the US Alternative Airplay charts and #8 on the US Adult Alternative Songs chart.

"You can't ever say no the first time around. So I never said no and I ended up never *looking like myself. If you are a new artist, you are fair game for everybody, and you're not going to gain any power until the second time around. I can now look back on it and learn from the experience. I have yet to do a nine-hour photo shoot this time around."* [85]

– Fiona Apple

When it came time for the music video, Fiona had learned from her past criminal mistakes, and she hired her then-boyfriend, filmmaker Paul Thomas Anderson, to direct not only the "Fast as You Can" video but all three videos from the record.

The video showed Apple singing around a house and a subway. As it was filmed using a vintage hand-cranked camera, Apple's mouth movements often do not match the lyrics. Who cares? The once sullen girl was having fun! And people liked that! Hence, the 2000 Billboard Music Awards nominated it for "Best Pop Clip of the Year."

• Limp

"I was standing there in this uncomfortable situation, when I realised my nails were digging into my palms. I got a pen and,

without even thinking, wrote down the words,
'When I think of it, my fingers turn to fists.'
I was miles away from trying to write a song,
but there it was, staring at me. And kind of
poetic, too. I was like, `Thank you.
I can use that.'" [37]

– Fiona Apple

For the second single, Fiona pushed out her more aggressive side due to her ongoing battles with relationships. It fittingly dropped the day after Valentine's, February 15th, 2000.

"I tend to see lots of similarities between the
relationships that I have with many different
people. So I mould all those people that have
one similarity into one persona, and I write
a song about that one person. Everything
comes from real people, and everything comes
from real things that happen. All the feelings
are things that I feel. But in terms of who
I'm talking to in the songs, it's all mixed up.
'Limp' is about every single boyfriend I've
had. And my parents, all my teachers, lots of
friends, specific ones. I don't want to name

names, but I could. I know exactly who I'm singing about" [112]

– Fiona Apple

For the music video, Fiona puts on a business outfit and partakes in odd activities around her house, such as putting together a puzzle or watching herself on TV. Sadly, the song was not as successful as much of her other work, and it has been largely forgotten. However, fans often reference the lyric *"You fondle my trigger, then you blame my gun,"* as one of her best.

• Paper Bag

The final *Pawn* single was "Paper Bag" (released June 2000), which has an interesting backstory. While driving in the car with her father during the *Tidal* recordings, Fiona was having a terrible day. That is until she saw a dove flying around outside the window. She took it to mean something positive but was soon disappointed as the lyrics tell:

"It came down near. So did a weary tear. I thought it was a bird. But it was just a paper bag." [37]

– "Paper Bag" lyrics

All's well that ends well, as the incident inspired perhaps *Pawn's* most accessible pop tune in which the music world effortlessly found its place. Rolling Stone ranked it the 29th Best Song of the Decade and the 382nd Greatest Song of all Time in 2021. It was nominated for the Best Female Rock Vocal Performance for the 43rd Grammy Awards in 2001 (losing to Sheryl Crow's "There Goes the Neighborhood"). And both *The Last Kiss* and *Bridesmaids* films featured "Paper Bag" on their soundtracks, which is interesting as Fiona was known to refuse licensing requests in the past. What changed?

"Let's not be too precious. Give me money!" [8]

– Fiona Apple

The Anderson-directed video is a ton of fun to watch, where Fiona prances around a 1940s scene surrounded by young boys dressed smartly, joining her with synchronised dance moves.

A little less fun was the lyric *"Hunger hurts but starving works,"* which has become a popular slogan in the eating disorder community, even once referenced in a published medical paper titled *"Hunger Hurts, but Starving Works: The Moral Conversion to Eating Disorders".*

Other Noteworthy Songs

The Japanese edition of *When the Pawn* came with two bonus tracks: Fiona's Beatles cover of "Across the Universe" and a live version of *Tidal's* "Never Is a Promise."

Twenty years after *When the Pawn*, Apple and King Princess collaborated on a new version of "I Know," which was released on January 25, 2019, for Spotify's RISE program.

"I fucked myself by writing all those songs when I was angry and hurt. Now, in order to live, I must rehash these memories all the time. Once the song starts, it's as though you have gotten drunk, and you can't help it. The room just starts spinning. But you wake up later and you're fine. When I come out of the song, I'm out of it." [7]

– Fiona Apple

5.2.
Relationship Status: Paul Thomas Anderson

"Every single relationship that you have is a completely different species of love. It's not the same thing, right? So for me, that never dies. It changes into a different kind of thing."[118]

– Fiona Apple

Throughout your early-career Fiona studies, you'll find a lot of *"Paul Thomas Anderson, Paul Thomas Anderson, Paul Thomas Anderson."* But who is Paul Thomas Anderson?

"He's impressed me so much that I want to impress him, and that makes your work drive go up."[119]

– Fiona Apple

Anderson is a powerhouse Hollywood director, the brains behind such modern classics as *Boogie Nights* (1997), *Magnolia* (1999), *Punch-Drunk Love* (2002), *There Will Be Blood* (2007), *The Master* (2012), *Inherent Vice* (2014), and *Licorice Pizza* (2021). The two met during a 1997 Rolling Stone cover shoot, and we can only imagine the electricity that buzzed behind the cameras. He was soon hired to sit in the director's chair for Apple's "Across the Universe" music video, and the two started dating that same year.

"He is a nitpicker like I've never seen before. But he'd get it right. And sometimes I'm a little half-assed about things. With the last album, I didn't realise what a joy it is to be able to put things together."[43]

– Fiona Apple

Their romantic relationship flourished, meshing with their creative partnership, which continued through numerous music videos. As we covered before, he was involved with every film piece from *When the Pawn*, giving Fiona a lot more control over her image, swerving away from the caricature pressed upon her during her *Tidal* days.

"Paul's going to do all my videos from now on. We used all the people from his movie crew, and it's all really fun. I don't have to wear any makeup or anybody else's clothes. No negligees!"[85]

– Fiona Apple

"She's learned so much. It's not a learning curve, it's a straight line. She's been able to gather information, process it, make sure she's not being lied to by the people around her, and really make her own record. I was able to pick up notebooks lying around and steal her lines."[43]

– Paul Thomas Anderson, Then–Boyfriend

Sadly, relationships are difficult. Or, in Fiona's words, "painful and chaotic". According to her, Paul had anger issues, which manifested into violent outbursts, including throwing a chair across a room and pushing her out of his car. Fiona became "fearful and numb" until they called it quits in 2002. However, the two appear to be on relatively good terms, and this is not the end of their work-related collaborations.

5.3.
Pawn Tour and Roseland Meltdown

"As a person who performs on stage, it's good to be emotionally open. If you mess with someone when they are in that state, it's like you're messing with an animal when it's eating."[22]

– Fiona Apple

In 2000, Fiona hit the road, touring *With the Pawn* across the USA with 33 shows. She also stopped off once in Vancouver, Canada, and once in Osaka, Japan.

"Everyone thinks, because my music is so personal, that it hurts me to get out there and expose myself. But it hurts more to keep it inside, because that's when I feel ashamed of who I am. You know, I spent all those years with people sending me into therapy saying I was crazy and I felt ashamed of what was inside. And this is my way of saying 'Fuck you.' I'm not ashamed; I'm emotional, I'm a freak. That's who I am. What's wrong with it?"[46]

– Fiona Apple

Like many points of Fiona's career, the most memorable show sticks out for undesirable reasons. It was February 29th, 2000, at the Roseland Ballroom, New York City, where equipment issues plagued her set. In front of a 3,000-strong audience, Fiona gradually melted down, apologising and tearing up until she cracked and stormed off stage, crying, refusing to come back on. The understandably disappointed crowd was left wondering what exactly happened.

"The short answer is that I'm a human being and I was reacting to life and overwhelmed and I just couldn't handle it. I mean, the simplest answer is that I started crying and I

could not physically stop crying. I couldn't. And it was just, like, ah, I gotta get out of here!"[120]

– Fiona Apple

Fiona also addressed the incident with a post on her website, which read:

"I'm so fucking sorry that I don't have whatever it takes to be professional in a situation like that. I feel like I let everyone down and made a fool of myself in front of everyone I respect. But I don't know what else I could have done."[121]

– Fiona Apple

Some fans were furious, but considering she managed to get through 10 songs over 40 minutes, and that this is the only example of Fiona ever walking off stage, it really isn't the most unforgivable story in rock history.

"I love Roseland the story because I remember... the world was done."[122]

– Fiona Apple

"It wasn't fun to have a meltdown and stop a show. I mean, that would make me cringe for years. But I don't want to take it back now, because I sit here and it's funny to me. I'll talk about Roseland forever. I could talk about the speech I made at the Video Music Awards. All the things that would be embarrassing or something, I'm fine with it. I have no shame about any of that stuff. And it delights me to look at that, to be like, 'Look, you thought that was the end of the world.' And it's not, it wasn't, so much so that I have not a bit of cringe in me about these things."[123]

– Fiona Apple

5.4.
Backseat Driver

A quick sidestep fact about Fiona: she doesn't drive. In truth, her half brother, Bran Maggart, used to live in her guesthouse and was hired as her designated driver.

"Really, like, I never know where I am. I can't get around by myself. I have a bit of anxiety about learning to drive. I just feel like I'd get really angry or I'd be so nervous of fucking causing an accident that I'd actually cause one. I know it's annoying for my friends, but it doesn't bother me."[43]

– Fiona Apple

5.5.
Working From Her Shell (part 1)

Three years between albums would be considered a lengthy break for some artists, but by no standard is it unreasonable. However, in terms of Fiona's catalogue, this gap proved to be significantly short. Indeed, as the years rolled by, the spaces between her records only grew longer with each release. After her *When the Pawn* tour, she moved to Los Angeles and six years passed before we heard original music from her again. But what did she get up to?

"Nothing. I really wasn't doing much at all [...] I kind of just decided to lie easy, and I got really dependent on television a little bit."[124]

– Fiona Apple

These vast distances between releases have become a sore point for many fans, and Fiona constantly has to justify her hermit reputation. As a result, we have collected more than enough quotes on the topic over the years, so here is a dump of the best:

"*I was thinking about that a lot lately because I didn't think that I was gonna get asked this so much. But once I have been asked this, I thought, man, I could have done so much! I could have gone to college! I wish I had more of a liar in me so I could say that, like, I've been working on a novel or something like that. I can't think of anything [...] I really didn't know if I was ever gonna do anything in this field again. I don't know why I always feel like that [...] It's a good sign when you feel, like, 'I just don't have anything else to write about.' I've already said everything. And that's a good thing I'm saying because that means that, you know, I've expressed everything. I've gotten everything out [...] I'm not that ambitious. I'm not that career-minded.*"[125]

– Fiona Apple

"I'm really good at intuiting what I need to do to be happy with whatever I create. I know when to stop myself. I know when to start. I know when you leave something alone. And I guess I just kinda indulge that completely. And so I just take my time."[126]

– Fiona Apple

"I have to see nothing wrong with it. I never feel like I have like writer's block or anything because I just think that the times when you're not writing are just as important. They're the times that you absorb things before you have anything."[127]

– Fiona Apple

"My relationship to solitude is always going to be really good."[45]

– Fiona Apple

"I hardly ever leave my house or my neighbourhood, really, and that's not a sad thing. I got my handful of friends in my handful of nice places that I like to go, and that's really enough for me."[128]

– Fiona Apple

"I'd say that I've been reclusive the last 34 years. That was my big thing as a kid, staying home from school. I've trained myself to be psychosomatically sick a lot. To this day, if I go to [LA club] Largo, which is a very comfortable place for me, I tell my brother, 'I have show stomach,' which feels like the flu. Anytime I go out, it is just something to deal with, even walking to the grocery store. If I'm supposed to go from one place to another place that isn't that comfortable, I usually don't go."[7]

– Fiona Apple

"I got a lot of shit too, like after the last album, from people that were close to me. 'You have to keep on working! You're being lazy! You have to get to the next thing! You're wasting what you've got! You've got this great opportunity!" And it's like, no, really, if I were to force myself to do it, then it would be crap."[129]

– Fiona Apple

"I could write another album in the next two months and be right back out here, or I could never write again. The songs I've written in the past have served a purpose. They were my way of dealing with my life. If I grow out of that, it's fine, and I'll figure out what to do next."[115]

– Fiona Apple

"It comes in seasons. Every single time I finish something, I have to resign myself to the fact that I might not write another song."[130]

– Fiona Apple

But none of this was entirely true, as Fiona did take a break from TV watching in 2002 to duet with Johnny Cash on a Simon & Garfunkel cover of "Bridge Over Troubled Water".

The song was included on Cash's final (non-posthumous) album, *American IV: The Man Comes Around*. It was Grammy nominated for Best Country Collaboration with Vocals.

"I'd listened to the first 'American Recording', and I was backstage at a concert—U2, I think—and Rick Rubin was there. I told him I really liked it. He said, 'We're doing another one; you should sing on it'. I got really excited, but about six months went by, and I felt like an idiot. I thought Rick had said that just to get rid of me. But one day, he called, and I went over to his house. Johnny Cash was there, and he was really nice. He'd already put down his vocals, and there was a camera crew there, and I didn't even know that I was gonna sing. I felt so nervous." [115]

– Fiona Apple

Assumedly from that same session, Apple and Cash covered Cat Stevens' "Father and Son", which surfaced after Johnny's death in 2003 on a boxset called *Unearthed*.

"[Harmonies are] not where my confidence lies. But I heard Johnny say to someone that he thought our voices went well together, so that's what I take from the experience."[131]

– Fiona Apple

Finally, in perhaps her most unusual move, Apple contributed to the *Christmas Calling* album with a magical cover of "Frosty the Snowman." This festive compilation also featured songs from Macy Gray, Tenacious D, and Sum 41.

Part Six
Extraordinary Machine

6.1.
Extraordinary History

The complex journey behind *Extraordinary Machine* means that we can't simply jump into the album and expect everything to make sense. Instead, our story begins slow, with many false starts and confusing strands, ultimately ending with not one but two very distinct records in our hands. But let's not speed ahead of ourselves.

"The first couple of years, I didn't have anything left in me to write about. That was a good thing, because it meant I'd done my job on the last batch of songs. I was riding a wave of independence. I wasn't trying to write. I just figured if the songs came to me,

they came to me, and if not, oh, well, it's been fun." [132]

– Fiona Apple

At one of their weekly lunches in 2002, Jon Brion told Apple about his recent split from his long-term girlfriend, comedian Mary Lynn Rajskub. The breakup was driving him crazy, primarily because Paul Thomas Anderson had hired him to score the film *Punch-Drunk Love*, which starred Mary Lynn Rajskub herself. Seeing his former partner's face on screen every day was too much, and he begged Apple to make another record, stating, "I need work that can save me." Fiona agreed along with some conditions, including recording without a deadline. Her label Epic gave their blessing, and off they went.

"I needed a kick in the ass anyway. I need to be pushed otherwise, I mean, I didn't even know six years went by. Ten years would have went by if I was left to do it on my own time." [133]

– Fiona Apple

Meeting at Ocean Way Recording, Fiona began sessions with only five songs written. This was a different method of songwriting for the artist, which turned out to be problematic compared to her usual style.

"I wasn't quite finished writing, and I wasn't quite sure I even wanted to go in and record again. So when we got there, I kind of froze. John would do a whole bunch of stuff as he does because he's really good at so many things, and he'll go in and he'll play every single instrument ten thousand different ways for ten thousand hours, and I'll go home as I like to do and then I'll come back and listen to things. And I know exactly what I like and exactly what I don't like and pick and choose out of it. That's what happened on the second record. On this record, I had no idea what I wanted, so it just basically became more of John's record. Which was great! The stuff he's done was great, and I was really proud of it." [134]

– Fiona Apple

The sessions picked up momentum and everyone appeared excited with the work. Engineer Tom Biller and our friend percussionist Matt Chamberlain soon joined the crew as they bounced from Paramour Mansion to Cello Studios in LA, and then flying off to London's Abbey Road Studios for strings. A release date of July 22nd, 2003 was prematurely announced.

Brion believed the album was completely done by May 2003, and a new release date was pencilled in as September 30th. However, it was soon reported that Brion and Apple were back in the studio for finishing touches, pushing the date to February 2004 and then a far less concrete "early 2004." And then... it just never came.

"I didn't know exactly what my vision was for the album, but I knew that I wasn't there. And I wasn't able to tell John what I wanted because I didn't know what I wanted." [134]

– Fiona Apple

After so much searching without finding creative satisfaction, Fiona's eventual solution was to rerecord the album with Mike Elizondo, who played bass on *When the Pawn*. Her confidence was not misplaced, as he'd made a huge name for himself on the hip-hop scene, producing and writing tracks on 50 Cent's *Get Rich or Die Tryin'* and Eminem's *The Marshall Mathers LP* and *The Eminem Show*.

"I got hooked up with Mike Elizondo, who really wanted to work with me. And this sounds horrible, I can't even remember how that even started! But I just know that he wanted to give it a try. He took some of the

tracks home with him, and he started from scratch, and he made some tracks of his own. I went in to hear him, and like, all of a sudden, I was like, okay, I know what I want now." [135]

– Fiona Apple

"She said, 'I have this batch of songs; I'd like to come up with different versions [...] I took a song at a time, learned it, then from scratch made different versions, different grooves. Fiona was open to experiment. There were no boundaries." [132]

– Mike Elizondo, Producer

Sadly, Sony was losing their patience. When Fiona proposed the new versions, the label demanded she submit each rerecorded song one by one for their approval, which knocked Fiona spinning flat to the floor.

"Everybody is saying that this is a big misunderstanding, and I don't think that we'll ever know exactly what the truth is. But I know what the truth is from my point of view. What happened is that I was told that, in order to do the songs, I would have to do one at a time and then hand it in to them and then they'd give me the money to do the next one [...] I was going back and forth in my head, going, 'should I do this, should I do this' and I went 'wait, this is ridiculous!' If I hand in something to them, then that implies that they're going to have a say in whether or not I get to do another one [...] so at that point, it just became too much of a drag for me, and I quit. I called my manager, and I said, 'just say that I'm not gonna do the album anymore.'" [134]

— Fiona Apple

6.2.
Leaky Machine

"I know what my part of the job is. I know that I write the songs, I know that I sing them, I know that I play them on the piano. I know that I have a feeling in my head—I have an intention with how they're supposed to come out—but I don't know how to articulate it, musically, with other instruments. [...] On Extraordinary Machine, I didn't know what I wanted, and I didn't help [Brion] at all. Maybe I'm just making up this memory, but I'm pretty sure he told me how frustrated he was with me. I imagine that he must have been because here we are, we're recording, and I was like, 'I don't know what I like; I don't know what I hate,' and it was a really scary place for me to be in. As a result of that, it came off more as a Jon Brion record, you know? I love it. I do. I'm delicate because I'm saying, 'Well, it turned out to be a Jon Brion record, so I wanted to do it again.' It's hard to say that without saying 'Jon took over,' like Jon threw up all over it. It's not that at all." [12]

– Fiona Apple

From as early as June 2004, tracks from Brion's version of *Extraordinary Machine* (known then as *Better Version of Me*) started to dribble online. Then around March 2005, CD quality rips suddenly flooded file-sharing programs, with 46,759 people sharing them. The Recording Industry Association of America intervened, with many hosts taking the songs down. Still, the word was out: a full new Fiona Apple album was available without any word from official sources. Everyone wanted answers, yet could only find different stories. For starters, Brion claimed Sony had shelved the record because there were no obvious singles.

"The record company wants 'Criminal' junior, and Fiona doesn't offer that up. She wrote that stuff when she was 16, and she's now in her mid-20s. She's extremely intelligent and writes this beautiful, really emotionally involved stuff that's very musical. Lots of chord changes, very involved melodies, intensely detailed lyrics. It's just not the obvious easy sell to them." [136]

– Jon Brion

Sony disagreed, somewhat correctly telling fans that Fiona was rerecording a selection of the songs. As for Fiona, when asked about a future release date, she reportedly responded with, *"You'll probably know before I do."*

"I lost track of what I was saying. I just walked away, and nobody really seemed to care until it got leaked." [12]

– Fiona Apple

To make matters even more complicated, listeners were more than happy with the leaked album they had, some even preferring the bootlegged versions to the eventual release. The New York Times found it a "fine counterbalance to a pop moment full of monolithic, self-righteous sincerity." Journal Now described it as "a work of daring and sophistication, as wildly imaginative as it is entertaining." And Pitchfork said, *"Extraordinary Machine* flaunts a quirky, cold-world cohesiveness that's as inviting as it is alienating."

We will go deeper into the differences between the two

versions in a later section, but for interest sake, here is the agreed-upon tracklisting from the leaked version of *Extraordinary Machine*:

1. Not About Love (3:46)
2. Red Red Red (3:30)
3. Get Him Back (4:32)
4. Better Version of Me (3:33)
5. Oh Well (3:51)
6. O' Sailor (6:25)
7. Used to Love Him (3:43)
8. Window (4:33)
9. Waltz (Better Than Fine) (3:45)
10. Extraordinary Machine (3:41)
11. Please Please Please (3:55)

TOTAL RUNTIME: 50:11

Meanwhile, Fiona was considering quitting the music business for good.

"I filled out an application to go be an intern at this place called Green Chimneys in upstate New York. It's a place where they do occupational therapy for kids, but they use farm animals. I'd been a volunteer a couple of years before for occupational therapy with kids, and I really enjoyed it. The fact that there were farm animals involved was really

cool. So I applied for an internship, which was going to be in the winter in upstate New York, for four to five months. I was really excited about it, and I was really sure that that's what I was going to do." [12]

– Fiona Apple

Thankfully for us, fans intervened...

6.3.
Free Fiona

"There was a time when I just kind of figured, like, well, I guess this is the way it's supposed to be, and I'll just go and do something else [...] Then those Free Fiona people just came right in and swooped me up." [137]

– Fiona Apple

Long before Free Britney, there was the Free Fiona movement. Started by a 21-year-old man named Dave Muscato, he took it upon himself to do everything he could to ensure *Extraordinary Machine* officially found its way into our homes. His first move was to create the website freefiona.com, which is still accessible today.

"I've loved her music ever since [Tidal] came out in 1996. I'm curious myself to hear it, but more importantly, I hate to see creativity and art oppressed by money issues. I understand that this is a business decision, not a personal one, but I think [Sony] is wrong. The album will sell if it's released. She has a strong enough fanbase that they'll make their money back, if that's their main concern." [136]

— Dave Muscato, Free Fiona Founder

Sony was quick to double down that they did not shelve the record, but it was too little too late, and the masses of Fiona fans came running. There were protests outside Sony's New York offices and around 1,500 apples were sent to Andrew Lack, CEO of Sony/BMG Music.

"They started sending apples to the executives at Sony. I don't really even know exactly the extent of what they did. They did a protest outside of Sony, I know that because I was in New York when that

happened, and basically they just started creating a lot of heat." [138]

– Fiona Apple

News of the support reached Fiona, and it moved her to try again. She got in contact with Sony to discuss the best way of finishing the album.

"I already got over all my sadness. It wasn't going to happen, I resigned myself to lying on the couch and I was all ready to do that. Then my manager, Steve, he said 'uh so there's, like, a protest going on with those Free Fiona people.' And I said, 'What Free Fiona people?' First of all, I think that it had a lot more to do with just the state of the music business than just me. I think that I was a really good case to focus on. But they set a goal, and they went, and they did it. And, I swear, I don't think that record company is going to say this at all, but I know the truth that they got my record out [...] They taught me a lesson that way." [137]

– Fiona Apple

"*My own personal feeling was, on one side, it was a little disheartening knowing there were these versions of the songs out there while we were working on the record. But on the other side, I looked at it as, it was very admirable, she has this amazing core of fans. The way they interpreted it was, the label isn't putting out her record, so we're going to do it for her. That's very admirable. But as time goes on, these fans will understand this is the album she wants to put out.*" [139]

– Mike Elizondo, Producer

"*I ran into the guy who started Free Fiona after a show in Chicago. He apologised to me! They didn't get the story quite right, but they did help me get my album out. I felt so bad that he had spent all this time thinking I was pissed at him. I had a physical urge to get down on the floor and kiss his shoes!*" [100]

– Fiona Apple

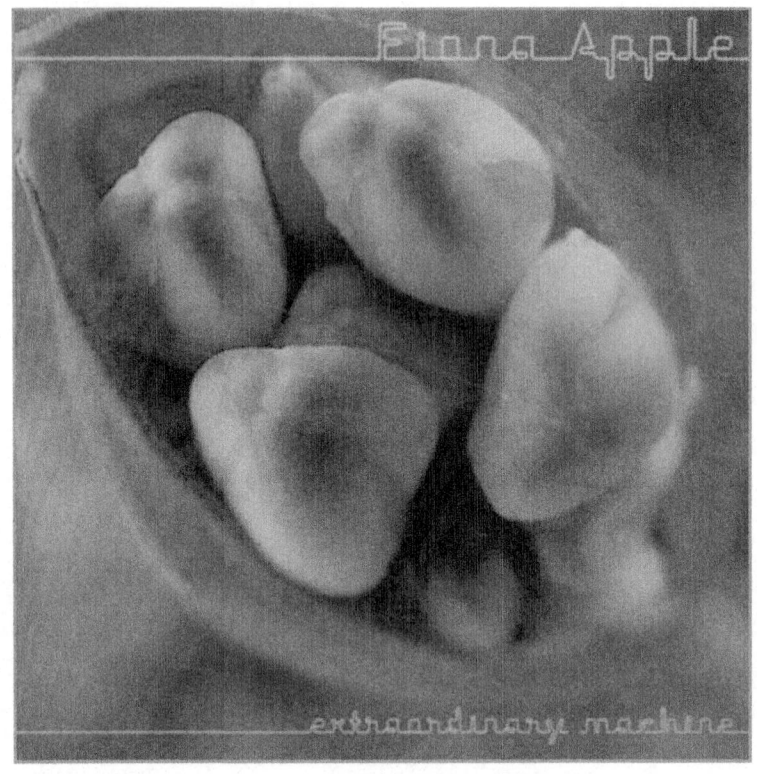

6.4.
Album: Extraordinary Machine (2005)

1. Extraordinary Machine *(3:44)*
(unchanged from Brion version)
2. Get Him Back *(5:26)*
(fourth single)
3. O' Sailor *(5:37)*
(first single)
4. Better Version of Me *(3:01)*
5. Tymps (The Sick in the Head Song) *(4:05)*
6. Parting Gift *(3:36)*
(second single)
7. Window *(5:33)*
8. Oh Well *(3:42)*
9. Please Please Please *(3:35)*
10. Red Red Red *(4:08)*
11. Not About Love *(4:21)*
(third single)
12. Waltz (Better than Fine) *(3:46)*
(unchanged from Brion version)

TOTAL RUNTIME: 50:34

"That's just a great album." [1]

– Fiona Apple

Six years since her last official release and after a completely different version leaked, Apple's "second third" album finally arrived on October 4, 2005. As before, it was released by Epic and Clean Slate. Recording took place in Phantom Studio behind Mike Elizondo's Westlake Village home.

Along with Elizondo, the album was coproduced by Brian Kehew, a member of the electronic duo The Moog Cookbook. His resume also boasts projects by Beck, Aretha Franklin, Talking Heads, Fleetwood Mac, Ramones, Morrissey, and Black Sabbath, to name a few. Questlove from The Roots contributed drums to "Get Him Back" and "Not About Love". *When the Pawn*'s Jim Keltner drummed on "Waltz (Better Than Fine)". Abe Laboriel Jr. (the drummer from Paul McCartney's band) took on the rest. Dave Way mixed the record.

Title

"It's called Extraordinary Machine because that was kind of like my hopeful pet name for myself. Give me anything, be mean to me, do whatever, anything life, do whatever. And it'll go through me, and it'll come out something nice." [140]

– Fiona Apple

"Not to be gross, but it's like a sort of creative mental form of, like, shitting. You know, taking things in and putting them out and leaving more room to take more things in, taking the nutrients in, whatever they are. Conversations with people or experiences or seasons or taking

all those nutrients in, what you need. Hopefully what you put out isn't shit, though. " [141]

– Fiona Apple

Sound

"I've got a bundle of songs of which I am exceedingly proud. And I'm excited to see how I handle the whole trip this time around, being that I'm finally at the point where I can call myself an adult without losing myself to the giggles. " [132]

– Fiona Apple

On paper, the sound of *Extraordinary Machine* seemed much the same old Fiona, and you may hear it being called anything from piano rock, art pop, alternative rock, chamber pop, jazz pop, or progressive pop. But beyond those usual genre suspects, there was a much notable quirkier edge to what she was going for.

"They're all about my boyfriend. Men are my bread and butter. It's what I live for! I have no shame about that. Being in nature and the

unspoken language between people and dogs and sex and relationships is what life is all about. Everything goes back to that." [142]

– Fiona Apple

Meanwhile, Fiona's lyrical content continued to mature. After having her life so fiercely thrust into the spotlight at such a young age, her emotional growth was temporarily stunted. However, on *Extraordinary Machine*, 27-year-old Apple appeared to be embracing adulthood while still pondering her signature themes. Identity. Alienation. Empowerment. And, of course, relationship dynamics, which many believe allude to her former partner Paul Thomas Anderson, a love which broke apart right about the time she started recording the album in 2002.

Artwork

"I like the picture. It's a cool picture and it's a way out of another photo shoot too." [143]

– Fiona Apple

The album cover is a close-up photograph of an agapanthus bud, which Apple snapped in her front yard.

"I just took the picture one day, and I really liked it. I don't know what they're called, stupidly. But the flower on the front is the same purple flower [at the back], just before it bloomed. And I liked how they looked like little fists." [144]

– Fiona Apple

Charts

With 94,000 copies sold in the first week, *Extraordinary Machine* debuted at seven in the U.S. Billboard 200 chart, Fiona earning her first top-ten album. However, the thrill didn't last, with the record losing almost 50% of its sales in the second week, tumbling down. This result accurately reflected the general consensus towards *Extraordinary Machine*, perhaps her most polarising release ever. Still, it has continued to sell, reaching one million copies in the U.S. by 2012.

Critical

With an 84 Metacritic score, there is no denying the success of *Extraordinary Machine*. Amazon.com led the praise with 100%, stating, "She shatters already sky-high expectations." Similarly, Entertainment Weekly's 100/100 rating lauded the new versions, with "The cleaner take on *Extraordinary Ma-*

chine is like a trip to a less cluttered haunted house, and Apple's more nuanced delivery sticks the knife in, but slowly. It's both charming and devastating." And then Rolling Stone gave it 80, going as far as to call this her "strongest and most detailed batch of songs yet."

However, not everyone was impressed, and the animosity usually came from those who preferred the leaked *Machine* over the official release. Slant changed their 80 score to 70 in light of the update, complaining that "not only have Brion's strings been replaced by an indescribably awkward alt-rock guitar riff and a misplaced drum beat, but Apple's vocals have lost all of their bite and passion. On Brion's work, she seemed hungry, ready to get back into it all. Here she retains the emotion that such a talented singer can muster on a good day but none of the rawness that signifies her best work." Pitchfork agreed with an unfairly low 62, saying that "the officially released version of *Extraordinary Machine* remains a decent-to-good album, one that showcases Apple's considerable vocal and key-pounding talents [...] The shame of it all is that Apple, after six years of silence, could've made a more definitive, progressive statement rather than something familiar and similar. And we've got the bootlegs to prove it."

Again, such opinions don't matter. For starters, it was nominated for the 2006 Best Pop Vocal Album Grammy Award (losing to Kelly Clarkson's *Breakaway*). And above this, it's about the persistence of the art. At the end of the year, Slant called it the Best Album of 2005, Rolling Stone number four, and Amazon number ten. Rolling Stone in particular has kept its love afloat, naming it the 49th Best Album of the 2000s in 2009, and the 444th Greatest Album of All Time in 2020.

What was happening was undeniable: people were finally taking Fiona seriously on an artistic level.

"I'm enjoying myself now. Like, people receive me for interviews, and they don't have that smirk look on their face anymore." [75]

– Fiona Apple

Singles

• O' Sailor

"O' Sailor" was the first single out door, released on August 16, 2005. Surprisingly, the song failed to chart, but the video was well-received by fans and critics alike.

"It's a ghost story. It's Fiona singing from a place where her lover has thrown her overboard and left her to sink, drown and die. She haunts this big, old ship. You don't know if the sailors are really there, or if she's there alone and they're memories that she's singing about. She's sort of there in spirit. I got really attached to the line [in the chorus], 'Letting it go by the boards', a phrase that sailors use

for throwing something overboard that they don't need" [145]

– Floria Sigismondi, Video Director

Floria Sigismondi was hired to direct the piece because Fiona was seeking the morbid style for which this artist was known. Such a talent is easily demonstrated by Sigismondi's incredible work with the White Stripes ("Blue Orchid") and Marilyn Manson ("The Beautiful People"). In the video, a ghostly Fiona sullenly glides around the ocean liner Queen Mary unnoticed by the ship's crew. The performance culminates into a strange dance sequence which was choreographed by Michael Rooney, the same mind behind the dancing in *When the Pawn*'s "Paper Bag".

The Music Video Production Company Awards were highly impressed with the clip, nominating it for eight prizes: "Director of the Year," "Art Direction," "Cinematography," "Choreography," "Styling," "Make-Up," "Direction of a Female Artist," and "Hair" (winning the last two).

• Parting Gift

The next single, "Parting Gift", dropped on August 16, 2005, and it was notable as the only brand new song that didn't exist on the leaked version. Fiona recorded her vocals in one take.

The music video was directed by Fiona's brother, Spencer Maggart (aka Brandon, Jr.). It's a simple piece of work where Apple sits at the piano and plays the song. Again, this track did not make any noise on the charts.

• Not About Love

"It has a lot of tempo changes in it, and it's this sort of like schizo song." [146]

– Fiona Apple

A curious pattern with Fiona's albums is that her third single often hits hardest. There was *Tidal's* "Criminal", *When the Pawn's* "Paper Bag", and now, the frantically exciting "Not About Love" song from *Extraordinary Machine* released January 2006.

Famously, this was the first *Extraordinary Machine* track that Apple performed live. Furthermore, we are, of course, dealing with two versions here. The one that leaked was well-loved already. Slant Magazine described it as "defiant, a poetic, regret-filled account of the morning after secrets were spilled," for example. This caused issues when the official version dropped with notable differences. Critics like Pitchfork Media were not impressed, stating, "On 'Not About Love' [...] Brion scored Apple's compositions no less extravagantly than his soundtracking work for the indie-film elite, applying dollops of lush orchestration [but] Elizondo hacks away Brion's embellishments [...] in his efforts to keep the spotlight fixed solely on her."

Thankfully, it was down to taste, and many preferred the new version. such as Seattle Weekly who observed, "Brion's busy cello keeps hounding Apple, getting in your ear while you're trying to figure out what the poor girl's trying to say [...] Elizondo, in contrast, merely pairs the piano with light-handed percussion, which creates drama—not melodrama, as per Brion."

"Some people may know that you and I shot a music video in [my] house for one of your songs. What was it called? 'Not About Love'? Which is a song about what?" [147]

– Zach Galifianakis

Like every single from *Extraordinary Machine*, "Not About Love" struggled to chart, but fans didn't care. Instead, they were far more invested in the music video, which starred her good friend, comedian Zach Galifianakis, in a rough, digital video type of home recording. In it, the two play a couple whose relationship is falling apart, but instead of Fiona singing, Zach lip-syncs the words (often reading them straight from paper). The clip proved popular on the internet.

"We just did the thing because we're all friends. I mean, I never really even learned the words to the song. And all of a sudden, I've gotten a bunch of emails from people telling me they've seen the video on TV and stuff like that, though I wouldn't be able to verify those claims because I don't even have cable." [146]

– Zach Galifianakis

"When Zach and [director] Michael [Blieden]

and I were making the video — we did it all at Zach's house in Venice — I was telling them, 'My secret hope in doing this is that it actually won't just be on the DualDisc. I hope it actually gets turned into a proper music video. Which was sort of a weird goal because the whole thing is pretty low-key. Basically, I'm with Zach the whole time, and he's singing, and I just sit there trying not to laugh. And not succeeding." [146]

– Fiona Apple

• Get Him Back

The fourth and final single was "Get Him Back", released on February 6, 2006. As is the case with the album, there was a lot more attention paid to the bootlegged version, especially with Brion's drum fill work. That said, Blender magazine did rank the official piece as the 35th Greatest Song of 2005. There was no video shot.

Other Noteworthy Songs

"There's a song called 'Better Version of Me' that is jam-packed with stuff from word-and-phrase origin books. Another called 'Red, Red, Red' is inspired by a book about optical illusions." [148]

– Fiona Apple

As previously noted, Fiona was perfectly content with two of the leaked Brion versions, and they made it onto the album unchanged. Those were "Extraordinary Machine" and "Waltz". The nine other Brion tracks were rebuilt from the ground up, except "Parting Gift," a new song recorded just for the updated version.

Fiona has expressed distaste towards the song "Please Please Please". In some ways, it can be compared to *Tidal's* "Criminal", whereby the label didn't hear a hit, and she tried to knock a quick single out. Fiona has gone on to call it her least favourite song of hers.

"It's just a song I wrote because the fucking album label fuckers were, like, 'You need another song.' [...] and I was, like, alright, I'll give you another song." [149]

– Fiona Apple

One major song that had Fiona groupies salivating was "Oh Well" due to Brion's announcement in 2003 that he cried when he first heard it. Sadly, those tears of heart-stirring were soon replaced by tears of frustration, as Brion later described the track as the album's "problem child".

"I feel like this is a good time to tell a funny story [...] so me and my brother we were going to get me a box radio and my boyfriend had just cheated on me with this starlet lady. She was all over every cover of every magazine and the most beautiful girl in the world. [...] So we go to this store to get our box radio [and we] go into those, like, RadioShack stores where it's, like, wall-to-wall ceiling-to-floor TVs [...] and I've just finished crying about the whole thing and we walk into the store and every TV screen from floor to ceiling, 360 degrees, has the girl's face on it. There was this moment of·like looking at each other, me and my brother, where we had to laugh for just like two seconds [...] and I still say that being the inspiration for ['Oh Well'] is the best work that little girl will ever do." [150]

– Fiona Apple

The German 2006 deluxe edition of *Extraordinary Machine* came with a bonus DVD, which included two new covers recorded live at Club Largo. The first was "River, Stay Away from My Door" written by Mort Dixon and Harry M. Woods in 1949, made extra famous by Frank Sinatra. The second was

"You Belong to Me" written by Billy Rose and Lee David, recorded by Irving Kaufman in 1926. The full list of DVD content below:

1. Not About Love *(video)*
2. Extraordinary Machine *(Live at Club Largo)*
3. River, Stay Away from My Door *(Live at Club Largo)*
4. Paper Bag *(Live at Club Largo)*
5. Fast as You Can *(Live at Club Largo)*
6. You Belong to Me *(Live at Club Largo)*
7. Parting Gift *(Live at the Jazz Factory)*

6.5.
Brion Issues?

"We never really had a conversation about it. It was assumed that I was going to be trying other things and he had moved on to other things, and I know he loves Mike, and he knew about me starting to do stuff with Mike. I'm sure that he just wants me to be happy with my songs. It would be more important for him to see me finally being able to make decisions. I don't think that I'm a perfectionist at all; I think that I'm sloppy. In my head, I'm always wearing sweatpants." [12]

– Fiona Apple

Naturally, the biggest question in industry circles was how Jon Brion felt about being replaced by Mike Elizondo as the *Extraordinary Machine* producer. Rumours told that this decision caused a rift, but Brion has never said as much. According to Wikipedia, he is quoted as saying:

"She rerecorded a bunch of stuff, but whatever, that's her business. I remain a fan and think she's great, and she shouldn't have to meet too much resistance." [151]

– Jon Brion, Producer

Elizondo verified the sentiments.

"Jon was not involved, but he was cool on all fronts." [132]

– Mike Elizondo, Producer

Instead, Brion appeared far more upset with the leaked version, which he claims was not his final work after all.

"There's music on there that wasn't even part of [what I recorded]. It's wrong. It's not like, 'I don't quite like the mix'. I wasn't happy with [the leak] cause I don't like those versions. It's stuff that doesn't

reflect what we recorded, for the most part, except for the stuff that's just her and an orchestra. That's just right. But as far as the rest of it, it doesn't reflect what I recorded." [152]

– Jon Brion, Producer

If there was any doubt about their friendship, Brion and Apple performed together at Largo the Friday evening just before the announcement of the official version. They continued to collaborate on various projects. Fiona has been especially open to officially releasing both versions and has even expressed a desire to finish the leaked arrangements with Brion one day.

"Then Jon and I can go in and mix them the way we want. I really think it would be cool to compare [the two versions]." [145]

– Fiona Apple

"I think that I actually got really lucky to have two versions of these songs. Nobody really gets to do that... not on purpose, anyway. And if somebody likes one or the other better, it doesn't make a difference to *me, really. I think it gives them both more attention. I lucked out a little bit"* [145]

– Fiona Apple

That said, it may be suspicious to note that this was the last time Brion and Apple worked together on a full album.

6.6.
Extraordinary Tour

"No matter what I do to prepare myself, almost every time I get ready to go onstage, I feel like, 'Are you fucking kidding me? I'm supposed to go on?' I have to say this to my brother every night out loud and he takes it. I'm like, 'I need to make you understand that it's ridiculous that I'm going out there.' Like, I have to go back home and sit on the couch. I have to go to the hotel room and turn on the TV. That is what I'm supposed to do. That's what I'm equipped to do.

That's what I'm in the mood to do,
like, every night." [153]

– Fiona Apple

Apple embarked on several short tours to support the re-cord without leaving the States. From November 22 to December 11 2005, she headlined her own shows before opening up for Coldplay on their *X&Y* tour, January 25 to March 5, 2006. After a short break, she headlined another quick tour from April 10, 2006 to October 29, 2006. Damien Rice and Davíd Garza supported her. Fiona later joined Nickel Creek on a small US tour in August 2007.

"God knows that a microphone stand needs to be my anchor, my crutch. I used to just never let go. And the first time I took the mic off the stand was because it fell off by accident. I just had no choice! After that I was, like, 'okay, well, give it a try', but I've been very shy on stage. It's taken a while for me to develop the kind of confidence and presence to be able to just let go and be uninhibited." [154]

– Fiona Apple

6.7.
Marriage Status: Lionel Deluy

"My ex-husband, Lionel Deluy, is a very good friend of mine, too. He's lovely. I was married very briefly to Lionel." [30]

– Fiona Apple

Lionel Deluy is a French fashion and celebrity photographer who snapped some promo shots of Fiona. The two married and then later divorced. This relationship was such a secret that many fans aren't even aware of it, let alone when it actually took place. However, as she noted, it occurred when she was "twenty-something"; hence, we can deduce it was loosely around this era.

6.8.
Relationship Status: Jonathan Ames

"There's so many reasons to make an album. But one of them is certainly to impress my boyfriend." [155]

– Fiona Apple

In 2006, Fiona attended a storytelling event at The Moth, New York, where writer Jonathan Ames was reading. He is known for his work in the New York Press as well as stories that became television shows (*Bored to Death*, *Blunt Talk*) and movies (*The Extra Man*, *You Were Never Really Here*). The two hit it off and were soon together, remaining in a relationship for four years. They tried again several years later, but things didn't work out.

"It was comforting to be held by him. It was really just about me thinking that I am not functional enough to be in a relationship, which I still kind of think. He hates it because he has a girlfriend now. I'll be like 'What do you guys do?' I just really want to know. Like, what does a functional girlfriend... like you guys go places? She cooks dinner? You know, seeing all the things actual women do because I don't know what the hell people do with me." [13]

– Fiona Apple

The reason for their split was never black and white, but reports suggest Ames was worried about Apple's drinking problems. Regardless, Apple has called Ames her kindest ex. For a borderline TMI view into their dynamic, consider reading the article *Fiona Apple's Art of Radical Sensitivity* found in The New Yorker.

6.9.
When the Paws

"[Janet] was found on the streets in Echo Park with a rope around her neck and bites on her ears. But somebody fed her and kept her on their front porch for a couple of weeks, and a friend of this woman who found her came to me and said, 'Do you want a dog?' And I said, 'Yeah!' And it was as easy as that." [144]

– Fiona Apple

Around her *Extraordinary Machine* era, Fioana became a dog-mommy to a pitbull-mix named Janet.

"She was somebody that I could concentrate on. And you're always helped when you help

someone else. It makes you feel stronger, and I think in that sense, I leaned on her by taking care of her. When I first got her, I wasn't good with affection with people, and I think that in a little way, my lack of having affection with people was driving me crazy. And when I got her, it really was just so soothing and therapeutic for me. And also, she's just fun. You can wrestle with her, you can cuddle with her, and she's just the sweetest thing in the world." [144]

– Fiona Apple

This sparked something in Fiona, and she became dedicated to caring for doggos.

"I think that I learned that I had a different kind of strength than I thought I did. That kind of motherly strength. Because when it can feel like you're actually responsible for something, for someone, and that someone trusts you and it's unconditional, well, it makes you feel proud of yourself. I didn't think that I would ever be able to turn the tables and take care of someone else" [144]

– Fiona Apple

Sadly, Janet was diagnosed with cancer and died when she was 14 years old in 2012. We'll cover that later, but for now, know that Fiona has since adopted another pup, a pit-bull-boxer mix named Mercy.

"When I was adopting [Mercy], I was like, 'This dog is too much for me. She's going to need too much attention and exercise and she's really smart.' But there was this part of me that was like, 'No, I am the person that can do all that.' I made this bet with myself: I can be the person to match up with this dog. I can get up every day, and match minds. I look at Mercy like she's the coolest lady in the world. And she chooses to be next to me." [45]

– Fiona Apple

For superfans, Fiona has let us know the other names she uses when referring to Mercy, which include Moosh, Moosey, Mushclay, and Mushkil (which means "difficult" in Hindi).

"Mercy is very emotionally intelligent. You see the wheels turning when something is going on. I could go out into the yard and cry by myself, and [Fiona's housemate] Zelda's dog Maddie will find me and lean on me with that big body, like, 'I'm sittin with you lady. I got you.' And I just don't believe it—how did she know! When I first stopped drinking, I was having lots of panic attacks. I didn't go to a rehab, but I rented a little apartment and went to see a doctor every day, and I brought Mercy with me. It was just me and Mercy for a month. Often, she would come over and lay her body on top of me to ground me, and she just wouldn't move. They make you feel important, which is good for mental health for everybody. They look at you, and they need you, and you're their person. Every morning, when Mercy and I go running, there's always a certain point where she looks up at me, and she's like: 'This is so fun. I love this. Isn't this so fun? I love you.' And there's just nothing better." [45]

– Fiona Apple

Fiona took her canine love to the next level by funding dog rescues, paying her brother Brian to pick up strays, and placing them in L.A. foster homes.

"We want to go and buy some land, and that's just going to be dogs and dogs and dogs. If nobody sees me for the next few years, just know I will be with dogs." [45]

– Fiona Apple

6.10.
Dietary
Requirements

"I'm a vegan, but I don't care if you're eating turkey in front of me. I'm not a preaching vegan." [135]

– Fiona Apple

Unsurprisingly. Fiona's love for animals extended to a vegan diet.

"[It's] just a principal thing." [156]

– Fiona Apple

Fiona went as far as to contribute a recipe for "Sweet-and-Sour Cheatmeatballs" to the PETA cookbook *Delicious Vegetarian Recipes from Your Favourite Stars* in 2002.

6.11.
Working From Her Shell (part 2)

"I sometimes think that I must time-travel, and I don't remember it. Like, I must be off climbing a mountain in a parallel universe. I can't remember writing any of the songs that I've written. I don't know what the hell I do with myself. I feel like I'm 100 years old. I can't tell you what I did today. I can't tell you what I did for seven years. I can't tell you. It happens so seamlessly. I'm just floating along, and seven years go by." [123]

– Fiona Apple

After the joy of a Fiona album, there was the inevitable comedown as we waited impatiently for new material. In the case of *Extraordinary Machine*, seven years would pass before a new album arrived. However, that is not to say that Fiona completely fell off the map, and there was a semi-consistent dribbling of recordings if you paid attention.

In the same year as *Extraordinary Machine* (2005), Fiona Apple's sister, Maude Maggart, released her third album *With Sweet Despair*. If you're lucky, your version will have a bonus 12th track, which should feature Fiona herself, except it could be one of two efforts. Some editions had the sisters cover "Sleeping Bee" (Harold Arlen, Truman Capote, 1954), while other editions had "It's Only a Paper Moon" (Harold Arlen, Yip Harburg, Billy Rose, 1933).

2006 proved to be quite an active year for our hermit. Firstly, Fiona repaid a favour to Zach Galifianakis by appearing on his joke song "Come On and Get It (Up in 'dem Guts)". It was featured in Zach's TV show *Dog Bites Man* where he played Alan Finger. In the song, Apple sings such profound lyrics as: *"If you show me your fanny pack, I'll show you my fanny."*

In the same year, she performed a fiery cover of Elvis Costello's 1986 hit "I Want You" during a VH1 tribute to the man himself, who joined the song on guitar. Rolling Stone were impressed, claiming she "metabolises every molecule of the song's poisoned atmosphere."

Danny Elfman rushed next in line, hiring Fiona to cover "Sally's Song" on the 2006 bonus disk for his *The Nightmare Before Christmas* soundtrack. Following this, Christophe Deluy ended Fiona's 2006 by duetting on the song "Still I". After which, Fiona took a deserved 2007 break.

However, she was back in 2008 with a live cover of the

well-loved 1946 song "Angel Eyes" written by Matt Dennis and Earl Brent. It's a jazz standard with many versions out there, including ones by Nat King Cole, Willie Nelson, Ray Charles, and Frank Sinatra. She then joined Davíd Garza for the song "Loveless", featured on his album *Dream Delay*.

In 2009, Fiona contributed two songs to the compilation tribute album to Cy Coleman. Those covers were "Why Try to Change Me Now" and "I Walk a Little Faster."

2010 rolled around, and Apple performed with Jon Brion in January, proving the two were still on good terms. It was a charity concert for the Haiti earthquake, named "Love and Haiti, Too: A Music Benefit". The two later released "So Sleepy" for the *Chickens in Love* compilation, also featuring the Punch Brothers. Every song on that album was written by the 826LA students, a Los Angeles–based nonprofit organisation aimed to raise money for those children's creative writing skills.

That same year, Fiona was featured on Margaret Cho's sixth album, *Cho Dependent*, on a song called "Hey Big Dog." Sadly, Fiona was not in the music video and was instead played by Cho as a dog.

The tribute album *Rave On Buddy Holly* was released in 2011, and Fiona gave us her version of "Everyday" with Jon Brion. So if you take that and everything else over this period, we could compile a decent album of Apple material! More than enough to satisfy even the thirstiest fan, right? Perhaps not. But for those who were itching for a new album, they were in luck. Seven years after *Extraordinary Machine*, *The Idler Wheel* was upon us.

Part Seven
The Idler Wheel

7.1.
Album: The Idler Wheel (2005)

FULL TITLE:
The Idler Wheel Is Wiser Than the Driver of the Screw and Whipping Cords Will Serve You More Than Ropes Will Ever Do

1. Every Single Night (3:29)
(first and only single)
2. Daredevil (3:28)
3. Valentine (3:32)
4. Jonathan (5:03)
5. Left Alone (4:50)
6. Werewolf (3:12)
7. Periphery (4:58)
8. Regret (5:17)
9. Anything We Want (4:40)
10. Hot Knife (4:02)
(featuring Maude Maggart)

TOTAL RUNTIME: 42:39

11. Largo (2:41)
(bonus track on digital editions)

TOTAL RUNTIME: 45:20

"It was very casual, and I wasn't fully admitting that I was making an album. I got to use the time in the studio to inspire me to finish other things rather than feel like I was finishing homework to hand in.

It wasn't a lot of pressure. And the record company didn't know I was doing it, so nobody was looking over my shoulder." [100]

– Fiona Apple

While the wait was long, Fiona was reportedly working on her fourth album from as early as 2008. However, due to the previous muddled lines with *Extraordinary Machine*, Apple kept the sessions top secret, recording her new songs in Stanley Studios (Los Feliz, California) and NBB studios (New York City).

As previously noted, Jon Brion was no longer driving the mixing desk, and instead, Apple placed her touring drummer, Charley Drayton, in that seat. It may seem like a strange choice to some, but his credentials speak louder words, having played with The Rolling Stones, Paul Simon, Neil Young, Miles Davis, Johnny Cash, Mariah Carey, Bob Dylan, Iggy Pop, Janet Jackson, and Courtney Love, to name a handful. Furthermore, you can hear his percussion brilliance loud and clear on this album.

"This one I love, even though there's a lot of pain that I went through during the making of it. I feel very sure of myself. Not that I'm so great, but that I'm right. Nobody can tell me that my song isn't done." [157]

– Fiona Apple

Between the two of them, they covered most of the soundscape. Fiona (credited as Feedy in the liner notes) took control of "field recording, loops, truck stomping, dance partner, thighs on 'Daredevil', percussion, piano, celeste, timpani on 'Hot Knife', voice strings, singing, artwork, bass keyboard, and production". Meanwhile, Drayton (credited as Seedy in the liner notes) was responsible for "kora, autoharp, truck stomping, dance partner, percussion, guitar, bouzouki, marimba, drum set, voice strings, thighs on 'Daredevil', field recording, pillow, voice of pain, baritone vocals, string harp, Teisco guitar, and production."

The producer John Would helped with the recording, and we will hear from him again. Dave Way mixed the record, as he did with *Extraordinary Machine*. Sebastian Steinberg played bass and was so impressive that he joined her touring band. Finally, Fiona's sister, Maude Maggart, appeared on "Hot Knife".

The album was completed in 2011 but Fiona delayed the release a further year as Epic were changing presidents and she did not want her record to get mixed up in those politics. The label eventually got themselves together, and in conjunction with Clean Slate, *The Idler Wheel* was released on June 19, 2012.

"[I'm] really, really happy, I felt like I can die now, I've done what I want, this is me." [8]

– Fiona Apple

Title

Back at it again with her elongated album titles. Like *When the Pawn*, Fiona found inspiration in one of her poems again, but this time had no intention of beating the world record. In full:

The Idler Wheel Is Wiser Than the Driver of the Screw and Whipping Cords Will Serve You More Than Ropes Will Ever Do

Fiona has said a lot about the title over the years. Here are a bunch of quotes:

"I came up with it in a total rush. After having stayed up all night on a deadline, it just came to me right after the sun rose. I didn't realise people would be like, 'Oh shit, another poem.' It just came out to be what it was. Sorry." [7]

– Fiona Apple

"If you think about it, the driver of the screw has one job and he is always trying to change things. But the idler wheel is there and has this great effect on what the gears do. The idler wheel knows the machine much better than just this one thing that's

performing this one task. For the second
line, I had read about whipping cords in a
nautical book that my last boyfriend had.
I read that when ropes get frayed at sea,
you can repair the frayed ends of the ropes
with whipping cords that are very strong.
This goes right back to the parenting thing.
If I had a kid, and I had a choice between
teaching somebody how to avoid trouble, or
teaching them how to get out of it, I'd teach
them how to get out of it." [7]

– Fiona Apple

"Being still in the middle of everything else
but being able to feel everything. [The idler
wheel] doesn't look like it's doing anything,
but I feel like it's connected to everything." [157]

– Fiona Apple

"Of course you're going to say ridiculous.
Because that's what you do with me, right?
I put out another long title because that's
what the title's supposed to be." [158]

– Fiona Apple

Artwork

Fiona created the mixed-media artwork, which many claim to be her best album cover yet. The chaotic lines and colours assemble to capture a feminine face, which is a decent representation of Fiona's creative approach. Curiously, very little information exists about the piece.

Sound

"I wanted to make everything as stark as possible, so you could hear everything." [158]

– Fiona Apple

With Drayton's drum expertise and Fiona's piano mastery, the organic percussion-driven sound on *Idler Wheel* should come as no surprise to anyone. In fact, there is not an electric instrument to be found anywhere on the recording. It is purely acoustic.

"We threw pebbles down [David Blaine's] garbage chute. We threw a big huge water bottle down the spiral staircase. We hit the big water tank he uses to drown in." [158]

– Fiona Apple

"On the first night of recording with Charley [Drayton], we walked by this bottle-making factory. The door was open and you could hear a machine running. We both had our recorders with us and we agreed that the sound would be good for the song 'Jonathan'. Juan, the guy working the night shift at the factory, let us walk through and record the sound of the machine. That was the moment where I said, 'Oh, we're not making demos, this is going to be it. Me and Charley are going to make a record right now.' And then it just got fun. On 'Anything We Want', I've been playing this stupid pipe thing live, but that sound was actually me at my desk with a pair of scissors, a tin full of burnt-cedar sashays, and a plastic cup. I was hitting everything with scissors and the cedar was flying all over the place." [7]

– Fiona Apple

With this in mind, the art pop genre remains strongly intact, while other labels thrown around include jazz pop, piano rock, dark cabaret, and piano blues.

"I felt we could take the same risk with sound as the songs were taking." [158]

– Fiona Apple

Lyrically...

"A lot of my earlier songs are blaming other people and never thinking that I ever did anything wrong, because I was always trying to be completely loyal and honest and pure. It's so nice to come to a place where you can see how you absolutely enabled all these things to happen. It makes you stop being angry at people. It makes you start being more empathetic." [158]

– Fiona Apple

The stripped back sound of *Idler Wheel* gave space for Fiona's emotions to shout louder than ever, and while her prose continued to mature per every record, her troubles with love and isolation still dominated her output. But even in her anger and gloom, there is an optimism to be found through her wit and ability to focus inward this round.

"I really let everything just get spit out. I would not second guess anything. There were songs I would write about breaking up with somebody before I broke up with them, months and months before I broke up with them. And I'd go back to that song, and now it makes sense why I wrote that." [158]

– Fiona Apple

Charts

Selling 72,000 copies in its first week, the album shot to number three on the Billboard 200, Fiona's highest success yet. She also hit number one on the US Alternative Albums and the US Rock Albums charts. Go Apple!

Critical

Meanwhile, Critical acclaim was **explosive**, to say the least. With an 89 aggregated score on Metacritic, she received full marks from the Los Angeles Times ("It's essential 2012 listening for anyone interested in popular music as art"), The A.V. Club ("It transmits each of those feelings in excruciating, frank, and lovely detail"), and Entertainment Weekly ("It isn't easy listening. But it's worth it"). Other notable observations came from Sputnikmusic's 90 score ("It is perhaps the most unforgettable work of her career"), Consequence's 90 ("one of the most daring pop records in recent history"), Chicago Tribune's 88 ("It makes for a raw, unsettling listen, tempered by shots of dark humour"), Paste Magazine's 84 ("To her immense credit, Apple never flinches at such uneasy insights and insoluble contradictions, which makes *The Idler Wheel* a tough but rewarding listen."), Tiny Mix Tapes' 80 ("There's no such thing as universal appeal, but *The Idler Wheel,* despite its brittle sound and frequent fury, is galactic, at the very least.") and Spin's 80 ("The unexpected triumph lies not in the spectacle of the singer raw-dogging her emotions, but in her total command of the anarchy that results").

For the sake of balance, we will note that not everyone was as floored. Rolling Stone's modest 70 justified itself with "There's not a single big, chewy hook on the album. Sometimes the songs drag... But Apple's kooky energy pushes through the slow spots". Meanwhile, PopMatters embarrassingly didn't get it, their 60 stating, "Half of the album is magnificent, and stylistically contradistinct, while the other half exists in some offbeat and off-putting terrain that will either elude its listeners or alienate them".

Fortunately, as time went on, the album only evolved within people's recollections. When 2012 was over, everyone was convinced, and the record was called the Album of the Year by Time Magazine, Stereogum, Spinner, and NPR. It also hit the top 5 in Consequence of Sound (2), Entertainment Weekly (2), USA Today (3), Pitchfork (3), Paste (4), and Rolling Stone (5). This momentum carried the record to the end of the decade too, as Pitchfork called it the 5th Best Album of the 2010s while Rolling Stone has since called it the 213rd Best Album of All Time.

The Idler Wheel was nominated for the 2013 Grammy Award for Best Alternative Album but lost to *Making Mirrors* by Gotye, which is ridiculous by anyone's standards.

Singles

• Every Single Night

The first and only single from *The Idler Wheel* was the opening track, "Every Single Night". Released April 24, 2012, the stark celesta and marimba composition proved too out there for the charts, although it did hit 72 on the Billboard Japan Hot 100, Fiona's first entry there.

The lack of commercial appeal meant nothing as the critics worshipped it. Billboard called the song a "triumphant comeback" as a "childlike and eerie" piece. Allmusic said it was "Fiona Apple at her purest, and that's plenty complicated". Idolator labelled it a "delicate and quirky track".

A music video directed by Joseph Cahill accompanied the single. Through various surreal scenes, Fiona walks the streets of Paris, moves like a puppet on strings, shares a bed with a bull-headed man, feeds an alligator, has snails crawling over her body, and wears a squid like a hat. The Guardian compared the theatrics to Lady Gaga, while Rolling Stone said, "It's sort of like her breakthrough video for 1996's 'Criminal,' if it took place at a wildlife preserve instead of a seedy house party."

"I told [director] Joey [Cahill] just to come up with a bunch of things and do things to

me and put me in situations and surprise me. One thing I wanted to have happen was to be covered in snails. I laid in a bed of soil and they put snails all over me. And then they brought in shit that I would not have asked for. He put a dead squid on my head. I used to love to put snails on my arm. I have a bunch of pictures. I used to put half a watermelon out in my yard overnight and then go out there in the middle of the night and take pictures of them, like macro pictures of the snails sipping the watermelon. I would love to sit there and put them on my arm. I don't know, it just helped me think. I really like snails a lot." [159]

– Fiona Apple

The song has stayed alive through other artist's interest. Panic! at the Disco tried to sample the song for their 2013 single "Miss Jackson", which was originally called "Bad Apple" after the singer. Fiona listened to the song, then rejected the rights, which infuriated frontman Brendon Urie so much that he publicly called her a bitch.

"The reason I didn't give it to them—besides the fact that I don't remember it, so it probably wasn't that great to me—is because this other guy had just used a sample of that same song and had signed to my label. He'd already made a big video with that song in the background. And then Panic! at the Disco asked, and I was like, 'Wow, I can't believe they even asked me.' Usually people just go ahead and use it. I was just trying to not shit all over somebody else's sampling of my song by doing it twice, but [Brandon Urie] called me a bitch. Which I think is hilarious." [160]

– Fiona Apple

You can hear sampled version on REVOLT's YouTube video titled *"Panic! At The Disco's Brendon Urie Opens Up About Nixed Fiona Apple Sample, Band's New Approach"*.

Meanwhile, Lil Nas X bypassed any such resistance by not asking for permission when he used the sample on 2018's "Kim Jong" from his *Nasarati* mixtape. Fiona responded by asking:

"Hey, where's my money, you cute little guy?" [161]

– Fiona Apple

Other Noteworthy Songs

"'Periphery' could have been on an old album. It was a song that I had tried to do [earlier], but it had just not really worked out. Everything else was written for The Idler Wheel. There were a few things that were written a few years ago. 'Valentine' was written a few years ago, 'Jonathan' was written when I first started going out with Jonathan [Ames]. I don't remember writing any of it. That's probably just because it happens gradually. " [13]

– Fiona Apple

While "Hot Knife"was never an official single, it quickly shot up as the standout piece from the album, glorified as the favourite by critics and fans alike (on a personal note, it is this author's favourite Apple song too!). Aware of its potential, Fiona released a promotional video for the song, where basic shots were split-screened next to one another, perfectly reflecting the vocal layering provided by Fiona and her sister, Maude Maggart. Perhaps surprising to some, she hired her ex, Paul Thomas Anderson, to direct the clip.

"That was the most amazing experience that

I wasn't expecting it to be. I knew it was going to be great, because I knew that I love when [Maude and I] sing harmony together. But on that song, we sing the same line over and over and over and over and over and over and over again. It's not looped at all. It's totally live the whole time. And we're singing into the same mic and looking into each other's eyes, and you have to be so, so in tune with each other. It was like the most intimate sister time I'd ever had ever with her. " [162]

– Fiona Apple

Rolling Stone dubbed "Hot Knife" as the 12th Best Song of the year. American Songwriters preferred "Every Single Night" placing it as the 7th. Pitchfork argued that "Werewolf" was the 9th best (featuring the lyric that this biography is named after).

Speaking of "Werewolf", this song features the line "But you were such a super guy". Why?

"Oh my God, that is a reference to the movie The Big Lebowski, when she says 'you such a super lady.' " [163]

– Fiona Apple

"Left Alone" features the line *the ants weigh more than the elephants*," which Fiona states is her favourite lyric that she's ever written.

"I saw a David Attenborough special [...] where he was saying literally in a given area, if an elephant is standing there, the ants in that area or the insects in that area put together would outweigh the weight of that one elephant. And I just thought, well, it's true in nature, it's true outside, and it's true inside."'' [164]

– Fiona Apple

The Idler Wheel song analysis would not be complete without mentioning the song "Jonathan". As an obvious ode to her then-boyfriend, Jonathan Ames, the two broke up the same week she finished the record. Lucky timing for him as he got a love song instead of a hate song.

"I just finished writing an album. I can't write an album about you now." [157]

– Fiona Apple

Reportedly, when Fiona told Jonathan about the song, his first question was, "Is my name in it?"

The Deluxe edition DVD features "Every Single Night", "Anything We Want", "Fast as You Can", "A Mistake", and "Sleep to Dream", each performed live at Fiona's SXSW performance (March 14, 2012).

7.2.
Club Largo

Fiona talks about Club Largo a lot, but where is it? Los Angeles, of course! Known for its musical performances and comedy shows, Jon Brion regularly takes a Friday night residency here. Largo owner Mark Flanagan gave Fiona much encouragement when it came to releasing *Extraordinary Machine*.

"You know, I really owe Flanny. He really stepped in and gave me a pep talk: 'No, you can't let them change it.' Flanny is a cornucopia of goodness in my life." [142]

— Fiona Apple

Fiona is so smitten with the venue that she wrote the song "Largo" dedicated to it, which can be found as an *Idler Wheel* bonus track. Here she cleverly sings *"When over the rainbow's too far, go to Lar-go to Lar-go to Largo."*

The song also mentions Watkins Family Hour, a bluegrass musical collaborative of which Fiona is a member.

7.3.
Please Please Knees

"I like Venice, but L.A. is ugly. I would kill myself if I had to look out the window and see some places in L.A. every day." [7]

– Fiona Apple

When *Idler Wheel* was done but Epic Records was between presidents, Fiona Apple went through a rough patch where she "just spiralled downward, and everything looked bad". To combat her depression, she started to climb a hill near her home in Venice for eight hours a day, every day. This well-meaning activity destroyed her knees until she could no longer walk.

"Something about that was a rite of passage. I think it's really healthy to lose things or to give things up for a while, to deprive yourself of certain things. It's always a good learning experience because I felt like it really was like, 'I must learn to walk again.' I had to walk out all that stuff, and I knew it was stupid, and I kept on walking" [158]

– Fiona Apple

After months of therapy, she got back on her feet.

7.4.
Zen and the Art of Apple Maintenance

"Meditation is about letting things arise and fall away again—and not judging the thoughts that are in your mind, but just letting them go by. This was a huge deal for me when I first started meditating." [45]

– Fiona Apple

In 2011, Fiona attended a Vipassana meditation course, which consists of mediation from 5am to 9pm and where speaking is strictly forbidden.

"*I remember being told: 'When there is agitation, look where there is no agitation.' So if you have agitation inside, then go and look at a tree. It's not agitated. It's doing what it needs to do. Go and watch the ants work when they're gathering crumbs. Just look at something that's working and let it ground you.*" [45]

– Fiona Apple

This proved to be just another step that Fiona took to gradually heal her soul as she got older.

"*I don't have that need for the world to understand me anymore.*" [165]

– Fiona Apple

7.5.
Idler Tour
(Featuring Drug Busts and Dying Dogs)

"Usually I just try to pretend I'm by myself, because I think that gives the best show. I would rather watch somebody actually going through something." [158]

– Fiona Apple

When *The Idler Wheel* was presented to Epic Records, Fiona ensured they knew that they either accepted this record on artistic terms or did not get it at all. Having learned from the *Extraordinary Machine* turmoil, everyone agreed, and she went about developing a plan to promote *Idler Wheel* in ways in which she felt comfortable.

"*I've known Fiona since she was 17. So knowing who she is and how her process is and how that connection has been made between her listeners and her, it was the only thing that made sense to do.*" [166]

– Adam Slater, Manager

The primary approach was through intimate shows, which started with NPR and Pitchfork's South by Southwest show-cases on March 14 and 15, 2012. Here, Fiona debuted new songs which quickly found their way onto the internet, building a sensational buzz around her thirsty fanbase. A small tour followed around the USA, where Fiona continued to drip information and songs to the small crowds of around 550 per sold-out venue. The idea was to connect to fans on a more personal basis, and it worked.

On June 18, one day before *Idler Wheel* hit the stores, Fiona appeared on Late Night with Jimmy Fallon. Here she sang with the Roots as her backing band, performing "Anything We Want" as well as "Let Me Roll It", a Paul McCartney cover celebrating the former Beatles' 70th birthday.

The very next day, *Idler Wheel* landed and Fiona embarked on a much bigger tour than the one before, playing 28 shows around The States and Canada. After a short break, she took off around the USA again from September 9 to October 21, 2012, with 30 more gigs.

On her way to her Texas show on the 19th of September, Fiona's bus was stopped by the police in Sierra Blanca. A sniffer dog found small amounts of marijuana and hashish. Fiona was arrested and held at Hudspeth County Jail. Her show was postponed, but she was eventually released on a $10,000 bond.

The "Free Fiona" and "Criminal" jokes were abundant. Her partner in crime and bassist Sebastian Steinberg was arrested with her and later stated that her time in the cell featured "her best vocal performance ever". This incident places her among the many celebrities who were busted at the exact same spot, including Willie Nelson, Snoop Dogg, and Armie Hammer.

Fiona had her sights set on Latin America, but after returning home from the previous leg of her tour, she found that her 14-year-old pit bull, Janet, was incredibly sick, her health worsening from Addison's disease and a chest tumour.

"Janet has been the most consistent relationship of my adult life, and that is just a fact. We've lived in numerous houses, and jumped a few makeshift families, but it's always really been the two of us. [She is] my best friend and my mother and my daughter, my benefactor, and the one who taught me what love is." [167]

– Fiona Apple

Fiona cancelled her Latin American tour to be with Janet during her last days.

"*I can't come to South America. Not now. She doesn't even want to go for walks anymore. I will not be the woman who puts her career above love and friendship.*" [167]

– Fiona Apple

7.6.
Relationship Status: Louis C.K.

"I don't want to get into always talking about these men, but with Louis C.K., he did say that I can talk about whatever I want to talk about." [19]

– Fiona Apple

The exact dates are not public knowledge, but at some point before here, Fiona Apple dated stand-up comedian Louis C.K. Their partnership was so brief that the media hardly picked up on it until 2017 when C.K. admitted to incidents of sexual misconduct. Considering the topic was so close to Fiona's soul, she offered her thoughts.

"I know he's got such a great brain, and he understands why he did that shit. I feel robbed that he's not giving us what he thinks about that. And the fact that he's complaining about the money he lost, and that tired joke of, 'Hey, how's everybody's 2020? Did everybody have a great year?' That was a bad joke when it was done the first time, but it's not even a joke. The one thing I will say about that situation is that the women he harassed continue to be harassed by his little bros. By the little Louis bros. Fuck you, Louis bros. And fuck him for not even just acknowledging that. And for the record, he didn't apologise." [19]

– Fiona Apple

"I can't tell you how many men have advised me not to apologise because 'it makes you look weak.' [Louis] recently said something like, 'Women are really good at seeming like they're okay when they're not okay.' And that's true, but don't you fucking act *like their discomfort and not-okay-ness wasn't exactly what got you off. I am a very forgiving person. But I cannot forgive someone who cannot acknowledge what needs to be forgiven."* [19]

— Fiona Apple

7.7.
Sobering
Decisions

Whether prescribed meds, alcoholic crutches, or marijuana arrests, intoxicating substances built a slide beneath Fiona to assist her stresses until a slippery slope fell beneath her.

"I got drunk when I was 5. Everybody gets drunk before they're 21." [80]

– Fiona Apple

Rewind, and like so many of our lives, the story starts with her parents. More specifically, her father who had a severe alcohol dependence. A four-year-old Fiona remembers one night that ended in dad's bloodied face after a fight with a cab driver.

Still, Fiona never considered herself an alcoholic, even if she went through a phase of drinking vodka alone every night until she passed out. Rather, a much bigger issue appeared to be the psychopharmaceuticals that doctors slapped into her mouth.

"I had been put on an antipsychotic. Nobody who is not psychotic should be put on an antipsychotic. I'm not psychotic and I don't have schizophrenia and I'm not bipolar; I've only been diagnosed with OCD and complex developmental PTSD. But I was put on one when I was in this mental state." [30]

– Fiona Apple

These meds were to counter "complex developmental post-traumatic stress disorder" and her frequent night terrors, but according to Fiona, the dosage was "way too high." Mood swings followed that were so severe that she got an MRI to rule out a pituitary tumour. When Apple realised it was her medications, she began the arduous task of weaning herself off of them.

"The period [...] was such a horrible group of months because of all of the withdrawal I ended up being in from getting off of some medications. I was like, 'I need to do this now, before I have to go into rehearsals and go on the road, and do all this stuff,'

thinking that the world was going to be normal. I was like, 'I need to be on the right medications, and in order to do that, I need to get off the wrong ones.'" [30]

– Fiona Apple

Eventually, Fiona found the strength to give up the booze too, which she credits to the #MeToo movement.

"With everything that was going on in the news, everything that I'd been burying under drink – and for a time drugs, but mainly drink – for many years, you couldn't just bury it any more. It was poking through, but I was so numbed that I couldn't really understand what was poking through. I finally felt like, I gotta be clear-eyed now, I have to face this shit. I think of myself all these years as someone who speaks honestly and faces all this stuff but no, no, no, no. Not really. It'll be a battle for ever for all of us to keep on facing all that stuff." [89]

– Fiona Apple

Unsurprisingly, once her mental chemicals were rebalanced without the dependence on external substances, she started to feel much stronger.

"I know a lot of it has to do with stopping drinking. I was keeping myself in a stupor so I wouldn't have to deal with things and keeping myself drunk so I could be able to pretend certain things. That's a big thing that happens if you're a heavy drinker. If it's an everyday thing and then you stop, so many memories come back. You didn't even realise what you were trying to push down until you stop pushing it down. It all comes out and then you're like, 'Oh fuck, give me the vodka again.' It's hard, but I feel so much more sure of myself because I'm sober." [19]

– Fiona Apple

"It's gotten a lot better, again, since I quit drinking. So much better. So much less anxiety. I was really overmedicated." [30]

– Fiona Apple

But perhaps the funniest part of this story came many years before, when she sat through a life-changing night with Quentin Tarantino and Paul Thomas Anderson. On a bunch of cocaine, she listened to the two powerhouse directors detail their successes at hyperspeed for hours on end, an ordeal she described as "excruciating".

"Every addict should just get locked in a private movie theatre with Q.T. and P.T.A. on coke, and they'll never want to do it again." [168]

– Fiona Apple

For some far more pleasant conversations, search for the *"Fiona Apple and Quentin Tarantino – Iconoclasts"* documentary on YouTube.

"My favourite part of not drinking is that when people tell me things, I remember them. Evolutionarily, positive experiences and neutral experiences aren't really that important to remember. But scary and traumatic experiences are important to remember. So with our lizard brain, all those years thinking that you're making yourself numb to the trauma that you went through

and you feel like it's all just a fog, the thing that happens is that you just don't end up absorbing all the good and neutral things. All you have is this fuzzy dull pain of these cloudy memories of trauma. And then when you stop drinking, those cloudy trauma memories become very clear, and it becomes very very scary and it's really hard to get through. I'm still trying to get through it. But it is kind of fucking worth it because when people tell me things about their lives, I don't feel like an asshole anymore the next day for not remembering the details, you know? I can be a better friend, and that is worth everything." [169]

– Fiona Apple

"What fires wires together? If you keep on having these negative thoughts or being angry all the time, then that area of your brain is going to get stronger. Even when now there have been times that I've just felt so, so bad, I can take myself out of it for a moment and go: 'You watch, you've felt this way before, you're going to feel great again. And then you're going to feel terrible again, and then you're going to feel great again.' And when you're feeling this way, at least know that there's value in it. Just as much value in your suffering as in your pleasure." [158]

– Fiona Apple

7.8.
Working From Her Shell (part 3)

"Most of the things that I do are completely inspired by laziness." [170]

– Fiona Apple

Zip back a couple of months to May 8, 2012, and Fiona could be found on Sara Watkins' second album, *Sun Midnight Sun*. The song in question was a cover of Felice and Boudleaux Bryant's song, "You're the One I Love".

In November of that same year, a song titled "Dull Tool" leaked online, confirmed to be an Apple song written for the soundtrack to Judd Apatow's romantic comedy *This is 40*. As a long-time fan, Apatow was blown away by her contribution.

"I didn't know she would write anything. The song was perfect, and I knew exactly where to put it." [171]

– Judd Apatow,
Director of *This is 40*

Unfortunately, Epic Records was less enthusiastic. According to various sources, her label did not permit "Dull Tool" to appear on the soundtrack and retaliated by ceasing the promotion of *Idler Wheel*. Naturally, this infuriated Fiona. Despite the issues, the song appeared in the film but was not released separately. The response was warm, with Universal submitting the song to the Academy Awards, setting Apple up for her first Oscar nomination. Sadly, she did not make the finalists.

After a very active year, Fiona's notorious hibernation cycle began. However, if you kept focus, a patter of new material appeared in some strange places. In 2013, a cover of "Pure Imagination" was released, a song originally found in the 1971 version of *Willy Wonka & the Chocolate Factory*, written by Leslie Bricusse and Anthony Newley, sung by Gene Wilder as Willy Wonka. The reason for this production was to assist a clip for Chipotle advertising their new app. The dark animation went by the name "The Scarecrow," which drives a hard anti-factory farming message.

"Chipotle was in a big rush and they initially wanted Frank Ocean, but he screwed up

his voice. And they wanted to use 'Pure Imagination', a song I wanted to do in a show when I was 18 but was too afraid to. I didn't want Gene Wilder to be upset about that song being sung by some idiot. I thought that I had the best chance of doing it well. This is the absolute truth: The only person that I care what they think of the Chipotle commercial is Gene Wilder." [172]

– Fiona Apple

In 2014, Fiona's side career as a soundtrack artist continued strong. The show *The Affair* hired her skills for the title sequence in a song called "Container". It's a one-minute eleven-second a cappella piece, fitting the show's haunting themes perfectly. In 2019, Fiona returned to the drama series to cover the Waterboys' "Whole of the Moon".

"Fiona Apple has been my favourite songwriter since I was sixteen. I am honoured and humbled that she has chosen to lend her talent to our opening title sequence. If our show can approach one-tenth of the depth and complexity of her *song, I'll be very happy."* [173]

– Sarah Treem, Creator and Executive Producer of The Affair

2014 marched on as Fiona and her sister, Maude Maggart, covered Anton Karas' "I'm in the Middle of a Riddle." The song was featured on the Valentine's Day-themed compilation *Sweetheart 2014.*

Over the following five years, you'd be lucky to get a new Fiona song whatsoever, but every now and then, something would pop-up. In 2016, she made an appearance on Andrew Bird's tenth album, *Are You Serious*, on the song "Left Handed Kisses".

"My inclination was to write a song about why I can't write a simple love song. The song began as an internal dialogue. At first, it was just my voice. Then another voice came creeping in and I thought 'this should be a duet if I can find the right person.' I needed to find someone really indicting. [And Fiona] was totally committed. The session was a long whiskey-fueled night. Unhinged, for sure. All worth it, of course. I can't write simple love songs. People are complex." [173]

– Andrew Bird

It was released as the record's second single, complete with a wonderfully simple video in which the two sit on opposite chairs, singing at one another.

In 2017, Fiona released a protest song against Donald Trump for the Women's March on Washington. It was titled "Tiny Hands" for short, or "We Don't Want Your Tiny Hands, Anywhere Near Our Underpants" for long. It samples Trump's infamous "grab 'em by the pussy" quote.

In 2018, Fiona Apple joined the vocalist for Garbage, Shirley Manson, at the Girl School Festival in Los Angeles. As a festival driven by female talent, Fiona used this opportunity to wear a shirt that read "KNEEL, PORTNOW", a commentary against Grammy head Neil Portnow's statement that women needed to "step up" if they wanted more Grammy nominations. The two performed a cover of Lesley Gore's "You Don't Own Me". Manson was suitably starstruck.

"When I got the opportunity to sing with Fiona, it was one of the most spectacular experiences of my life. And to just go to rehearsal and watch her walk in the door, step to the mic, open her mouth, and without any effect, without any great mic, without any trickery, the sound of that voice coming out of that tiny little body with no stress, no strain, was just spectacular. I have talked about her from the moment she emerged; I have followed her career with great ardour. And I couldn't admire her more [...] She's a once-in-a-lifetime artist with the voice of God." [174]

– Shirley Manson

"She walked into the door for rehearsal, then I saw her, it was like such a love scene in a movie where everything slows down and we were moving towards each other in slow motion. I was engulfed in this incredible euphoria. I really believe Fiona has the best voice of any white female artist over the last 20 or 30 years, so to get to sing with her was just off the fucking charts. I think all the women felt empowered by her presence there. She is a woman of great integrity and she's also incredibly punk rock. And it's so peculiar because it comes out of this tiny little singer. She's so slight and unassuming and quiet, and yet she has this incredible rebellious streak in her. I felt like all the women in the room thought, 'Yeah, we can take the next step – and that next step is some action." [175]

– Shirley Manson

Another two years passed before "I Can't Wait to Meet You" appeared on the 2018 compilation album, *Hopes & Dreams: The Lullaby Project.* As a cover of the Solangie Jimenez/Thomas Cabaniss song, it fit perfectly into the album's theme of the bond between parent and child. Soon following, she was featured in *Echo in the Canyon,* a documentary all about L.A.'s Laurel Canyon scene in the 60s.

One year later, in 2019, Fiona Apple joined the long list of artists who covered "Don't Worry 'bout Me", originally written by Rube Bloom and Ted Koehler. Fiona's version was a collaboration with the Mildred Snitzer Orchestra and actor Jeff Goldblum, featured on the latter's album, *I Shouldn't Be Telling You This.*

As previously mentioned, 2019 was also the year when King Princess released a new version of *When the Pawn*'s "I Know". Apple was heavily involved with the rerecording, which was released as part of Spotify's RISE program.

But even with that tasty little collection of morsels, fans were starving for a solid chunk of Fiona output. Which, thankfully, we received in a big big way the very next year...

Part Eight
Fetch the Bolt Cutters

8.1.
Album: Fetch the Bolt Cutters (2020)

1. I Want You to Love Me (3:56)
2. Shameika (4:08)
(first and only single)
3. Fetch the Bolt Cutters (4:58)
(featuring Cara Delevingne)
4. Under the Table (3:20)
5. Relay (4:50)
(samples "My Kettle, My Cats" by Sebastian Steinberg)
6. Rack of His (3:42)
7. Newspaper (5:32)
(featuring Maude Maggart)
8. Ladies (5:25)
*(music by Sebastian Steinberg and David Garza,
featuring Maude Maggart)*
9. Heavy Balloon (3:26)
10. Cosmonauts (4:00)
11. For Her (2:43)
12. Drumset (2:40)
13. On I Go (3:09)

TOTAL RUNTIME: 51:49

"Making my first album, [I would go to the studio] from 1pm to 9pm every day. While everybody else put together the arrangements, [I was] just sitting there being like, 'When do I sing? When do I sing?' The difference between [then and now], me being like, 'Oh, I think I'd like to play

that thing on this. Okay, I can go do that right now.' It makes me feel like I wasn't ever given a chance to be a musician before. Because you'd have to do everything in the studio, and I'm not good at doing things in front of people under pressure." [176]

– Fiona Apple

First announced using sign language, Fiona Apple's fifth studio album was released on April 17, 2020, during the COVID pandemic. That noted, it was in the works for around five years, even if the 2015 sessions at Sonic Ranch in Texas were distracted by playing with dogs, watching films, and taking magic mushrooms.

"There were quite a few months where we didn't record [...] So there wasn't an official start, but it really started when we started redoing stuff in the house." [19]

– Fiona Apple

The sessions gained speed once Fiona moved the recording to her home in Venice Beach, the "womb of where I've developed into an adult". Here, she felt comfortable to take far more control than usual, credited as the producer, along with her bandmates: bassist Sebastian Steinberg (also on *The Idler*

Wheel), multi-instrumentality Davíd Garza (her guitarist from the *Extraordinary Machine* tour), and drummer Amy Aileen Wood (Fiona's touring drummer).

Recordings mostly took place in Apple's house (Los Angeles) but saw other sessions at Stanley (Los Angeles), Sonic Ranch (Tornillo, Texas), and Waystation (Los Angeles).

Any additional familiar faces? Yes! John Would, who helped record *The Idler Wheel*. This round he took on some keyboard duties as well as engineering. Dave Way also helped with the recording and some mixing, a job he has been assigned to since *Extraordinary Machine*. Bob Ludwig mastered the thing. He is a multiple-Grammy award-winning engineer known for over 3,000 credits, including works with Led Zeppelin, Lou Reed, Metallica, Queen, Jimi Hendrix, Paul McCartney, Nirvana, Bruce Springsteen, and Daft Punk.

"We started first trying to be a band and to have me build my confidence up as a musician, because it was really low a few years ago. It's funny, I've never been able to jam with people. I've always been too shy to try, which is not a good way to be. If you grow up and you're praised a lot for being special, rather than for making an effort, you end up later on in life being afraid. I would get into situations where I don't even want to try because if I don't end up being special, then I don't value my own effort as

much as I should. I put together 'the band' in February of 2015 so that we could just jam, so I could learn how to feel as free as I do singing when I'm playing stuff. I don't think I ever got there, but it was good enough for me to start recording with the band." [19]

– Fiona Apple

Title

"I guess the message in the whole record is just: fetch the fucking bolt cutters and get yourself out of the situation you're in, whatever it is that you don't like. Even if you can't do it physically." [19]

– Fiona Apple

While the meaning behind the title may be profound, "Fetch the Bolt Cutters" was born from much simpler origins: the TV show *The Fall*. Here, Gillian Anderson's character casually says the phrase when examining a crime scene involving the torture of a woman.

"My housemate Zelda and I were watching the show The Fall starring Gillian Anderson and we're just eating dinner [...] there's a scene where she was going to rescue a young girl from where she thought she was, locked behind this door, and they were supposed to wait for backup and she just sort of throws away this line, and she says 'fetch the bolt cutters'. I just shot from the couch because I was, like, 'this is exactly what my record's gonna be called!' and I wrote on the chalkboard. I got a tattoo!" [177]

– Fiona Apple

When the album was released, Gillian tweeted an animated GIF of the scene as acknowledgement.

Of course, when the entire world went into lockdown, the title took on an even deeper meaning, many of us wishing we could simply cut our way out of that situation. Fiona echoed these sentiments.

"I was always able to leave before, and I chose not to. And funny enough, right when I'm like 'I'm fetching the bolt cutters! I'm

gonna leave this house!' It's like, 'Nope! No you're not!'" [178]

– Fiona Apple

Then again, we can all thank Fiona we had this playful record to keep us company during those hard times! But, of course, there was also no *Bolt Cutters* tour for this reason.

Themes

Fiona Apple has jokingly referred to *Fetch the Bolt Cutters* as "House Music" purely because it is a loose concept album about her Venice Beach home.

"I moved into this house in 2000, and I've always felt like [it] doesn't want me to go anywhere. So I'm like, 'All right, I'm going to give you what you want, house. I know you deserve to be the record. I'm going to make you the record.' This is where I feel comfortable. My boyfriend at the time, Jamie, really pushed for me to get it set up here so I could record by myself. Once he pushed for that to happen and Amy taught

me how to do GarageBand, it was like the universe opened up." [176]

– Fiona Apple

"I want to repay this house by making it the music. Because it has been my mother, really; it's been the home of all the music. It's been the womb of everything, for all these years. It's been the womb of where I've developed into an adult. And so I really felt like it's an instrument in itself, it's the microphone: The house is the microphone, the house is the ambiance, the house is a member of the band." [178]

– Fiona Apple

Yet despite the theme of reclusiveness, the album is far more about breaking free, as the title tells you. It is yet another evolution in Fiona's signature anger-fueled motion, where she conquers the shackles of her past while doing so with a flair of humour more blatant than any album before.

"You get your point across a lot better with a little bit of humour. And so much of humour is just familiarity, being able to relate to something. It's a good way to communicate." [179]

– Fiona Apple

"I don't really think of myself as funny, but I laugh a lot. I laugh a fucking lot." [19]

– Fiona Apple

Another strong current underlying these songs is about the unification of women and what it is to be a female in the current political climate. This theme is a notable step for Fiona, who has struggled around women in the past.

"My middle school experience is still so important to me mainly because that is where my relationship to women started getting fucked up. It's awful how many memories where a popular girl says to my friend, 'Okay, you can be friends with Fiona, or you can be friends with me, choose.' And I never got chosen." [180]

– Fiona Apple

"Boys can be mean but it's just kind of stupid mean. I'm not traumatised by boys bullying me. I'm more traumatised by girls rolling their eyes at me. I got silenced a lot. I silenced myself because I was afraid of the other girls saying I wasn't cool." [181]

– Fiona Apple

"I remember my grandmother used to talk about my grandfather and his mistress. And his mistress actually was his wife for the rest of his life. They were married for 50 years. But to [my grandmother], she was always mad at this mistress. And it was always like, 'Man, she didn't do it. Our grandfather did it. Your husband cheated on you. She just fell in love with some guy. Then they were together forever afterwards and had a family. Be mad at the right person, don't feel mad at the wrong person.' So, this album is a lot of not letting men pit us against each other or keep us separate from each other so they can control the message." [181]

– Fiona Apple

"There's always hope for women.
*We **are** the hope in the world."* [182]

– Fiona Apple

Sound

"What's funny is that so much of the stuff that I did on the record is stuff that I can't actually do. Like, I would try to do certain percussion things, and I'm not a percussion-ist. I wouldn't hire me as a percussionist! But I wanted to be the one to do certain things, or I was the only one that was here. So I'd just do take after take until I'd get something right. For touring and stuff, of course, I'll have to actually learn how to do the things I did, but wow, it's just a big, messy making of a record. Messy, messy." [19]

– Fiona Apple

The sound is, without a doubt, the album's primary focal point due to its giant stride away from what we've come to expect from an Apple record. The approach has a traditional sense, whereby vocal chants and unconventional percussion rhythms hit on a deeper spiritual level, coming across more improvised than a polished work. According to all accounts, anyone could bang on anything to produce a sound, and it would be considered. There are many examples, but understandably, the percussion choice that the press spoke about the most was Fiona's choice to tap on her dead dog Janet's bones.

"I found a stove top in the alley that's somewhere around here. Oh, there's a metal butterfly that I'm playing. It's the sound on 'Fetch the Bolt Cutters,' the higher 'clink, clink.' I found it outside of this elementary school in the grass. So that's kind of random." [19]

– Fiona Apple

Band member Davíd Garza added:

"She wanted to start from the ground. For her, the ground is rhythm. It felt more like a sculpture being built than an album being made." [1]

– Davíd Garza, Band Member

"I've been in the business for so long, and my favourite thing is drums. I have a very, very big memory—and I don't have many big memories—of going to see the movie Tap, with Gregory Hines. During one scene, he's in jail, and there's some water dripping down, and he starts tap dancing. I just like that feeling of: 'I'm in charge, I can do whatever I want.'" [7]

– Fiona Apple

We can owe *Bolt Cutter*'s shift to Fiona's willingness to experiment. This included using technology that Fiona was unfamiliar with, such as GarageBand and her iPhone, leading to "mistakes" that solidified to shape the record.

"Honestly, I would press record, and I would get so nervous, and I wouldn't have planned out what part I was going to do or what I was going to play. I'd just be like, 'I'll add something. I'll do whatever I feel.' So I'd press record, and after, I'd scramble to find drumsticks or to pick a keyboard, and most often I would forget to close the door. So the

dogs would hear something, and they'd bark, or something outside would happen. But then I'd play it back, and I'd feel like those barks kind of worked. It didn't bother me." [19]

– Fiona Apple

A good example can be found in "On I Go", where Fiona messed up a beat, cursing herself with an "Ah, fuck, shit." The blunder remains on the final recording.

"I've stopped trying to be a singer, actually. I have fun with my voice, but I'm not trying to make it pretty all the time. I'm not trying to convince anybody I'm a singer. It just turned out to be another instrument." [19]

– Fiona Apple

Artwork

The haphazard DIY aesthetic of the cover art weirdly fits the music as perfectly as possible. Fellow album contributor David Garza put it together.

"That face is very much me. I just wanted to be like, 'Hey, guess what? I'm back! Here are some songs. Want to listen to the music, huh? Hi, hi, hi, hi." [19]

– Fiona Apple

Perhaps more notable would be the reverse cover notes, which acknowledge the indigenous land. Fiona further clarified the decision to mention these:

"The reason why the album cover says 'This album was made on unceded Tongva and Mescalero Apache and Suma territories.' [...] these are people who are an afterthought. They got $2 billion in the stimulus, which is more than they've gotten before, but it's not going to be enough. They are so dependent on their elders and on each other to maintain their culture. This is a really, really dangerous time for them. So I wanted to acknowledge the lands. How are we ever going to be able to heal and join communities and be respectful of each other if we can't acknowledge the simple truth that this is

not our land? Not acknowledging things is nothing less than disrespectful." [19]

– Fiona Apple

"[Native American activist] Eryn [Wise] and I had been talking about doing land acknowledgments. She wanted to start this project, which I think is amazingly smart. When artists go on tour, they acknowledge the unseen lands that they're performing on and educate people about the tribes that lived on those territories." [19]

– Fiona Apple

This act of acknowledgement has become more commonplace in later years, making one wonder how much of a role Fiona played in that.

Charts

Selling 44,000 copies and hitting number 4 on the Billboard 200, *Fetch the Bolt Cutters* gave Fiona her third consecutive top 10 record. It was her second-highest debuting release, beneath only *The Idler Wheel*, which reached number 3. The album also hit number 1 on the Billboard Top Alternative Albums and Top Rock Albums. Canada, Portugal, and Denmark welcomed it into their top 10.

Critical

As for the critical reaction, somehow, *Fetch the Bolt Cutters* climbed far above everything Fiona had achieved before. The sheer number of publications that gave the record full marks is almost unheard of, including The New York Times ("daring in a new way, scrambling and shattering the pop-song structures that once grounded her"), The Guardian ("not so much an album as a sudden glorious eruption; after eight long years, an urgent desire to be heard"), Pitchfork ("a wildstyle symphony of the everyday, an unyielding masterpiece. No music has ever sounded quite like it"), and The Telegraph ("an album that conveys one woman's rage, vulnerability, confusion and wisdom in ways that we haven't quite heard before"), to name a few.

According to aggregate site Metacritic, not a pro review dared to rate lower than 8/10, leaving her with a whopping 98% score, making it the second-highest rated album in the website's history, below only Wadada Leo Smith's *Ten Freedom Summers* (99%).

Naturally, *Bolt Cutters* was the go-to crown for the end-of-year lists, too, named the Greatest Record of 2020 by Consequence of Sound, Entertainment Weekly, The Guardian, The New York Times, and Pitchfork. It hit the top three list with the Los Angeles Times (2), Rolling Stone (2), and Time (3).

Just quickly going back to Pitchfork, it is mindblowing to note that *Fetch the Bolt Cutters* was their first 10/10 perfect score since 2010's *My Beautiful Dark Twisted Fantasy* by Kanye West. At the time of publishing this book (first half of 2024), *Fetch the Bolt Cutters* remains the most recent album to achieve this status. Pitchfork's review itself is the website's most read on record.

"I haven't looked at stuff, but I know it was received well. Knowing that, and knowing how many fuck ups there are, and how imperfect everything is on it—I feel like I'm in a good relationship with the world. I feel like I showed up for a date with no makeup on, like I banged my head and I lost my tooth, and I showed up bloody and wearing half a T-shirt and one sock, and my date went, 'Hey, I like you, come on let's go. That's OK with me.' Which is a great feeling. I'll still kick myself for not being the kind of musician that I think is the cool way to be a musician. But I like that I finally went: 'I'm me. I'm going to accept what I am and try to make something good out of that.' I'm proud of myself for getting to a place where I could say: 'don't wait until you're perfect.'" [179]

– Fiona Apple

At the 63rd Annual Grammy Awards (2021), Fiona won Best Alternative Music Album and Best Rock Performance (with "Shameika"). However, she refused to attend out of protest against Dr. Luke, who was nominated for Record of the Year as Tyson Trax. Fiona considered this hypocritical due to the Grammys inviting Kesha to perform "Praying" at the ceremony three years earlier, a song which was about Dr. Luke sexually assaulting her. Instead, reportedly, Fiona slept through the ceremony.

"I don't know if anybody who's nominated can help having the thought: what would I do If I won? My vision was that I would just get up there with a sledgehammer, and I wouldn't say anything, I would take the Grammy and smash it into enough pieces to share, and I would invite all the ladies up. My second thought was, I wonder if I can get all these ladies to boycott this shit because of Dr Luke." [89]

– Fiona Apple

Another reason for Apple's Grammy absence appeared to revolve around her recent sobriety.

"I'm just not made for that kind of stuff anymore. I want to stay sober, and I can't do that sober. It doesn't feel safe to me to be in that kind of exposure, scrutiny, comparison to people." [184]

– Fiona Apple

Singles

• Shameika

Continuing to do things differently this round, Fiona ignored the standard single-release strategy before the record. However, "Shameika" became the lead single when it was dropped 10 days after the album, on April 27th. Keeping at this casual pacing, a video appeared several months later, on November 20th. It was an animated affair from Matthias Brown's pen, where illustrated lips sang the lyrics.

The song hit number 19 on the Billboard Adult Alternative Songs. This broke the record for the longest time between chart entries for an individual artist, as "Fast as You Can" was Apple's last entry on that chart two decades previous.

We've already touched on this song's significance during an earlier chapter, so let's recap with this quote:

"I've had this feeling for my whole life that nobody stands up for me. I have no memory of anybody ever getting in the way of somebody else being shitty to me, from when I was a kid to when I was an adult, except for this one moment where this girl walking by saw something going on, and leaned down and said, 'Hey, why do you care about them? You have potential.' I got to carry that in my head my whole life. When there was nobody on my side, I was able to call up those words." [16]

– Fiona Apple

The backstory of "Shameika" added even more depth to the already fantastic song. We covered the tale much earlier in this book, but to reiterate, a girl named Shameika stood up for Fiona against some bullies many decades back in school, stating that Apple "had potential". This compliment stuck with Fiona her whole life, and it eventually manifested into this song.

"Back then, I didn't know what potential meant, and Shameika wasn't gentle, and she wasn't my friend. But she got through to me, and I'll never see her again."

"Shameika" lyrics

Never see her again? Untrue! Fiona did see Shameika again, and it was all thanks to this very track. A teacher at St. Hilda's & St. Hugh's, Linda Kunhardt, heard the song, and as she was still in contact with Shameika. Kunhardt sent a message detailing the discovery to Shameika, who *"was, like, jaw unhinged"* in her own words.

"I was like, oh, my God, wait a minute! Because part of you is not believing this and then, it's obviously real because it's right in front of you. Because I'm listening on Apple Music, and I'm reading the words and everything." [185]

– Shameika

Linda Kunhardt then reached out to Fiona too, and Fiona was equally gobsmacked.

"When I first wrote the song, I was not entirely convinced she existed. Because I have this one memory and it's a very big memory for me. But maybe I created this person. My third-grade teacher, Linda Kunhardt, was my favourite teacher. I've kept in touch with her over the years. She read the New Yorker article, and the next day, she sent

me an email saying, 'I heard you wrote about Shameika' [...] she sent me a picture of her." [185]

– Fiona Apple

The story came full circle as Shameika and Fiona eventually sat down to video chat.

"We both cried. The word 'magical' was used a lot." [186]

– Fiona Apple

As it turns out, Shameika's life took her down a similar musician path. She was living in Virginia Beach as a rapper under the names Dollface or Chyna Doll. What's more, she can boast her fair share of success, including a feature on two songs from Blackstreet's *Level II* album (2003). Hence the conversation of a song collaboration was inevitable, and Fiona was more than keen. She ultimately rerecorded her hook for a new track called "Shameika Said".

"When we did the song, it was as though we had been together all of this time and talked every single day, like, this is my girl. We're never gonna be apart again. We're like connected spiritually." [186]

– Shameika

"Fiona's hair used to be all the way down to her ass, literally. You wouldn't dare see someone pick on this little girl. [I told her] Sweetie, you got potential. You don't have to worry about these girls, Fi. Come sit with me at my table. I've always been a protector of anyone else who's smaller, who can't defend themselves. I love to speak life on people." [186]

– Shameika

"This is the thing, that's who I am... I speak life on people. I do it now. It didn't stand out to me. But, oh my god, to her — and that's what we gotta realise as humans. Sometimes, we don't realise that something so small that you may not even, you might overlook it, it might be something major in someone else's life because of how it makes them feel." [185]

– Shameika

Other Noteworthy Songs

"Making this album has really helped me get through stuff, and I don't know if I can say that about my other albums." [19]

– Fiona Apple

Bolt Cutters is an album's album, a unified collection greater than the sum of its parts. As a result, the first five tracks collectively appeared on the Billboard Hot Rock Songs chart, which marks the first time she's ever appeared on that list.

"There are some chords I put into [the song] 'Fetch the Bolt Cutters,' but I didn't know what to do, so I decided to do C-A-G-E-D." [179]

– Fiona Apple

The title track's main talking point may be its guest star, model/actress Cara Delevingne, who sang backup on the chorus line while providing little meows.

"[Cara] and I have been text friends for years. But we've only hung out twice in person. I wanted her to sing on this one thing, but then she was only in town for a day.

And I was in a very sad place. So I was like, 'I don't feel up to anything. I'm sad.' She FaceTimed me and was like, 'Answer the phone. You're okay, everything's cool.' She was such a good friend to me in that moment that I felt really comfortable, and I was like, 'Okay, come on over, let's do it.' There's one line to sing: ['Fetch the bolt cutters'] She's got the British accent that went along with the way Gillian Anderson said it, so it was really funny actually when she started doing it. [...] I love her voice, and I just knew our voices would go really well together." [19]

– Fiona Apple

In the true spirit of the album, the barking of dogs was a happy interruption that Fiona left on the final recording.

"She brought her dogs, Leo and Alfie. And so all of our dogs—Maddie, Mercy, Leo, and Alfie—were in this room with the door closed and they're totally silent for the whole take of the song. And then, at the end of the song, they erupted. It was so perfect." [19]

– Fiona Apple

Interestingly, Fiona wrote many of the songs found on *Bolt Cutters* long before the project. One such example is "Rack of His" which features sister Maude Maggart's backing vocals, recorded while she was breastfeeding.

"Some of the songs I started writing years ago, [like] 'Rack of His.' I did a couple of versions. I almost put it on a couple of albums, but it was a completely different song." [19]

– Fiona Apple

Another noted oldie was "Relay", featuring the hook that Fiona wrote when she was 15 in response to the ever-present sexual assault she faced not long before that age: *"Evil is a relay sport, when the one who's burned turns to pass the torch"*.

"[If] you get burned by somebody, when the person who burns you doesn't acknowledge it—which rarely happens to people, acknowledging when they've burned you—it turns into you not knowing what to do with it. Then you just put it on somebody else. The assault when I was 12 made me think about *innocence and guilt and forgiveness. It made me think about a lot of big things. Because the first thing I did after it happened was pray for him.*" [19]

– Fiona Apple

Like the earlier-mentioned "Dull Tool," Fiona wrote "Cosmonauts" for the *This Is 40* soundtrack. Director Judd Apatow could not find a place for it in the movie, so we are lucky that Fiona held on and gave it to us here.

"['Cosmonauts' is] equally as great as 'Dull Tool'. It was heartbreaking not to put it in, but I'm sure it'll reach people at some point. It's a beautiful song." [19]

– Judd Apatow, Director of This Is 40

Another song that grabbed people's attention was "Under the Table" due to its humorous lyric, *"Kick me under the table all you want, I won't shut up."* It's about a dinner with a streaming music executive. But we can let Fiona tell that one.

"The funny thing about that song is that one of the people at that dinner who I had a problem with is now making more money off that song than I am. Some guy from

Spotify was there, and I don't know how they do what they do to us. It doesn't make any sense. Wasn't Napster supposed to be like, 'That's not allowed, don't do that.' And then they're like, 'Let us do it! You don't get to steal! We get to steal!' It's fucked up. I know I make less than they do off of work that I do, and I've never met them, and they don't do shit for me." [179]

– Fiona Apple

"I've never been to a dinner like that before or since, where there's like six wine glasses in a row out for each person, and they're tasting so many expensive wines. They open one $900 bottle of wine and let everybody sip it, and then they give you another glass. And everybody was talking about their accomplishments. We were all supposed to say something, and when it got to me, I was like: 'Hi, I'm Fiona Apple. I think it would be interesting if we talked a bit about what was going on in the world when each one of these *wines was made.' I thought that would be a great conversation for fucking rich people to have over expensive wines: What can this group of smart people do with that kind of conversation? Maybe something productive? No, let's just talk about the idiot book we wrote. Anyway I can't believe I'm still getting pissed off at that dinner. But it's nice to have your say."* [179]

– Fiona Apple

Speaking of backstories, another goodie rides behind "The Drumset Is Gone." While her breakup with Jonathan Ames was still fresh, she got drunk and proceeded to have a vicious argument with her bandmates. Afterwards, drummer Amy Aileen Wood packed up her kit and left for another gig, which Fiona mistook as a resignation from the band. Apple dealt with the incident the best way she knew how: by turning her emotions into a song.

"The drumset is gone, and the rug it was on, he's still here screaming at me."

– "The Drumset Is Gone" lyrics

It was recorded in one take.

But the line that sticks out in most fans' memories as perhaps the strongest from her entire career was in "For Her". This track was Fiona's response to the Supreme Court hearings of Brett Kavanaugh, where Apple shouts the distressing:

"Well, good morning! Good morning! You raped me in the same bed your daughter was born in!"

– "For Her" lyrics

"I really was not sure if I was gonna put 'For Her' on the record. I did so many versions, not even recording. It was really hard to even perform. My heart's starting to beat really fast just thinking about it. It's about another woman, and in a way, it's about Christine Blasey Ford [who alleged that Brett Kavanaugh assaulted her] and it's also about me. I didn't realise how much I was needing that song. I thought I was really writing it for other people. Then one time I was singing by myself and I happened to be standing on a mini trampoline. I was up at eye level with this picture frame and the sun was shining on it so I could see my reflection rather than the picture. I caught my reflection when I sang the line, 'You raped me...'

and I broke down, fell down on the trampoline. But it felt great. I felt like I finally believed myself!" [89]

– Fiona Apple

In these ways, it felt like *Bolt Cutters* was the most genuine
audio representation of Fiona we have received thus far.

"Although it's not so important to me what
happens because of this album, it is important to me the way I handle how I'm presented. In the past, so much stuff would
happen that just wasn't me. Which is excruciating, if the whole reason you were doing
anything was to be understood in the first
place, you know?" [19]

– Fiona Apple

8.2.
Fiona Has Ink

When the title *Fetch the Bolt Cutters* popped into Fiona's awareness, she was so excited that she permanently inked an image of bolt cutters on her right forearm.

"I made me. I claim my body. I can do what I want to my body. In some sense, it was an act of faith in myself because I got the tattoo before the record came out. So people could have hated it, and it could have been a disaster, but I wasn't going to wait to find that out before I tattooed it on myself because it doesn't matter what everybody else makes of it. What matters is that I did this. It was my own stamp of approval on myself. And it's a reminder: 'You got out

of this situation. What's the next barrier you got to get through?' It also goes back to Extraordinary Machine. I am the bolt cutters, an extraordinary machine. I can get myself free anytime. Plus, I just like how it looks. I've only gotten three tattoos in my life. " [179]

– Fiona Apple

Now seems like an apt time to discuss just what those other tattoos are. She tells Pitchfork:

"On the back of my neck, I've got my pets' names: Janet, Nancy, and Mercy. And I have what they call a 'tramp stamp,' but it looks cool. I got that tattoo for [ex-boyfriend] David Blaine, and for myself, because he had gotten a tattoo of my name on his shoulder, which is now covered up with the face of the devil, and I felt like I needed to do something in return. But I didn't feel right getting 'David' tattooed on me. I felt like we were kin, and he's always going to be in my family. So it's this symbol that I used to draw when I was a kid, and above it I put, 'Kin.' But it's half removed now, because another boyfriend didn't want me to have it. It's a faded tattoo now." [179]

– Fiona Apple

Below the Kin tattoo, you'll find the letters FHW, which stands for Fiona Has Wings.

8.3.
Relationship
Status: Jamie

"I had a boyfriend, Jamie, who helped me set up the recording. He's still my friend." [19]

– Fiona Apple

A round this era, Fiona seems to have had a brief relation-ship with a man named Jamie. Unlike many of her past romances, details are scarce to the point that it's difficult to find any information about the guy whatsoever! However, what we do know is that we can owe much of what *Bolt Cutters* became due to his ideas and encouragement. We've already used this quote, but it bears repeating:

"My boyfriend at the time, Jamie, really pushed for me to get it set up [at home] so

I could record by myself. Once he pushed for that to happen and Amy taught me how to do GarageBand, it was like the universe opened up." [19]

– Fiona Apple

8.4.
Antisocial Media

"I'm really scared of this shit." [187]

– Fiona Apple

One common question in our digital age of celebrity worship is: Does Fiona Apple have social media? According to every source, the answer is a deflated no.

"They want me to tweet now, but I don't. It doesn't feel natural to me. But I do find it actually more interesting to see people posting ridiculously mundane shit. I like to hear about what people had for breakfast or what they did all day. It's interesting because I don't know how other people live." [100]

– Fiona Apple

But that doesn't mean she doesn't get the word out when needed. Fiona's videos have been known to appear on her housemate's accounts across Twitter, Instagram, and Youtube @zeldahallman. The @fionaapplerocks fan account regularly receives exclusive content on Youtube and Tumblr. Her attorney, Scott Hechinger, delivers some messages via Twitter @ScottHech. Fiona does have an official Facebook page @fionaapple, but she has little (or nothing) to do with it, even if her official site, fiona-apple.com, redirects that way. There is another small debate that @dullt00l might be her on Instagram, but the consensus is that it is only a convincing fan account.

"Lately, I can spend a lot of time on the internet as a substitute for TV. This is part of the reason why I'm not a good girlfriend. You can't sit down with me and watch a movie. I hate being strapped down to stay with something. So when I watch TV, and TCM isn't on, I just switch channels and look at all the information about everything. The internet is perfect for that, which is why I didn't really want to get a computer in the first place. I thought, 'If I have a computer and know about this whole Google thing, I am not going to be able to sit still for a second; I'm going to think about something and

then have to look it up.' I have never bought myself a computer or a phone, but guys in my life have bought them for me, for whatever reason. So now I have them." [7]

– Fiona Apple

8.5.
Working From Her Shell (part 4)

We already know how this works. After the album cycle, Fiona's head pulls backward and, at the time of this book's release, we are still awaiting her divine return as the years keep falling falling falling...

Nevertheless, we know she's still out there with music on her mind because of her hired name appearing on other records.

Probably the biggest deal, if not for us then for Fiona, was her feature on Bob Dylan's thirty-ninth studio album, 2020's *Rough and Rowdy Ways*. Pay attention, and you'll hear her piano playing on the 17-minute epic "Murder Most Foul".

"I look down at my phone and see [long-time collaborator] Blake Mills texting me. I hadn't heard from Blake in months. And

he's like, 'So I'm working on something, I can't tell anybody about it, but we want you to come in and do something.' And I was like, 'Um, I can't, I'm busy.' And he was like, 'Can I call you?' So he called me and he goes, 'OK, it's Bob Dylan. Bob is asking if you will come here and record.' And I went: 'When?' And he went: 'Now.' And I said 'FUCK' so loud that I could hear people on the other end of the phone laughing." [179]

– Fiona Apple

"I told Bob I was really insecure about it, and he was really encouraging and nice. He was just like, 'You're not here to be perfect, you're here to be you.' To have Bob Dylan say that before my record came out was a huge deal for me. And I mean, this was like the one person I could have met who's alive right now where it actually would have meant something to me as a kid." [179]

– Fiona Apple

Perhaps not quite as exciting is when Sharon Van Etten celebrated the 10th anniversary of her *Epic* album by rereleasing it in 2021, except with each track covered by a different artist. Fiona was responsible for "Love More". Later that year, she provided another cover, this time a protest take on the Christmas classic "Silent Night", released as part of Phoebe Bridgers' Christmas EP *If We Make It Through December.* The song also features Matt Berninger of The National.

In 2022, Fiona Apple entered the *Lord of the Rings* world. She provided vocals on the song "Where the Shadows Lie", which closed the final episode of the first season of *The Lord of the Rings: The Rings of Power.* Written by Bear McCreary, Apple sings the Ring Verse inscribed upon the One Ring from Tolkien's books.

Most recently, Fiona offered her voice to singer Iron and Wine's 2024 album *Light Verse.* You can hear her on the song "All in Good Time."

8.6.
Relationship Status: Fiona Apple

"Nobody knows when exactly these songs were written or thereabout. And I'm certainly not going to help anybody find those things out! [...] Given the fact that these guys are people that I still talk to a lot and that I have very good nice warm feelings about now, I don't really think that I want to be specific about anything." [188]

– Fiona Apple

Fiona famously wears an open heart for all the world to see and is never shy about speaking about her past relationships. However, she does appreciate her privacy, which means we often only learn about her partners once they've already split.

"I'm starting to gather that people probably think that, like, I hate all the guys that I've known. These are songs are written in the moments when I'm feeling that way, but I used the song so I can get through those feelings. All of my relationships, they've ended badly in one way, but they've been reborn again. I'm friends with every ex-boyfriend I've got." [189]

– Fiona Apple

Regardless, so much of Fiona's artistic output focuses on her love life, and it's been fascinating (if not a little voyeuristic) to watch her thoughts on the matter evolve with her music.

"These days, I don't know who really likes me. I always assume most people are bullshitting me [...] Weird things will happen that end up hurting your feelings. I'll get a letter from somebody I knew a while ago, and I'll be really touched. Then I'll turn over the envelope and their business card falls out." [23]

– Fiona Apple

"I love seeing anybody in a good relation-ship. But I don't see that and want it for myself so much. I honestly have no interest in romance these days. I hope that's not me somewhere underneath being like, 'It's too painful to love,' because I don't like that. I don't get with that way of thinking of, 'I've been hurt before, so I'm not going to do it again.' You're new every time. Still, I've never been somebody who was like, 'I feel comfort-able when I have a boyfriend.' I just really want to be around the person." [179]

– Fiona Apple

"I really believe in completely being naive and having high hopes when meeting someone new. I can kind of re-do my stupidity or my naivete." [7]

– Fiona Apple

It's uncertain who, if anyone, Fiona is seeing now, but at least she appears to be in a strong relationship with the people who matter most: herself, and her fans.

"I'm definitely not always begging to be alone now. I just choose my company better. I'm not so antisocial. I'm not so hell-bent against having a boyfriend. It's just that my experience with that has taught me I'm more comfortable without it. But it doesn't mean that that always has to be my experience." [19]

– Fiona Apple

"If I have one success in my relationship history it's with the people who listen to my music. I think that they'll be there with me forever, and I'll be there with them forever. And I'm totally satisfied with that." [158]

– Fiona Apple

8.7.
Court Watcher

Forever propelled by a life of unpredictable choices, perhaps the most exciting recent Fiona development (at the time this book was published) is her ongoing investment in Courtwatch PG since 2021.

"Hello! I've come here today to tell you about my new makeup line! Yeah, I'm fucking kidding. About a year ago, I made a video saying 'fuck the Grammys, we don't care about the transparency there. What really matters is transparency in actual courtrooms.' That still matters." [190]

– Fiona Apple

Note: The above quote is pulled from a very cool video you can find on YouTube titled *"Keep Courts Virtual - Fiona Apple"*.

Here, Fiona simply explains how people could help the cause. It's worth the watch!

Ok, but what is Courtwatch PG? Founded by formerly incarcerated black women, Courtwatch PG is an organisation that trains volunteers to watch Maryland court hearings online.

"All we want is transparency, honesty, and to be able to watch the court like the Constitution says we can. We are not in 1822. We're in 2022. We should be able to watch court hearings by Zoom." [191]

– Dr. Carmen Johnson, Director of Courtwatch PG

Such an admirable idea naturally ran into opposition with the powers that be.

"How are we supposed to have our constitutional right to observe these courts or to help these people if we can't hear? And why did they take away this access right after this lawsuit was dropped? It really seems like they're retaliating against us. And if they're retaliating against us, I mean, man. What stupid, asshole babies, huh?" [192]

– Fiona Apple

"They're trying to shut us out, and you gotta question it. Like, why are you trying to shut us out? What don't you want us to see? There's people who are being held pretrial on nonviolent charges on bonds they can't afford, or no bond, and it's ruining families and fucking with futures that we need to help protect." [192]

– Fiona Apple

Thankfully, Fiona comes with her own star power, and after her involvement, they went from a handful of members to over 100. Furthermore, 7,000 signatures of support appeared in just two weeks, many with the added note "Fiona sent me."

"What did [Apple's shoutout] do? It took us from having one lone court watcher, to two weeks later, having 175 people send us email saying they wanted to learn more. They want to be a part of it. We still have emails that are coming in." [194]

– Qiana Johnson, Executive Director and Founder of Life After Release

"If you do it, you listen, and you learn to care about people that you would never have met before. That you would never have even known about before. And my god, we need more of that in this world. We need to care about the people that we don't know." [195]

– Fiona Apple

It has even been joked that she has done more promotion for Courtwatch PG than she has her own albums.

"I honestly hate doing stuff like this [...] I won't do it for my own music. It's not worth it. But this is important." [196]

– Fiona Apple

8.8.
Awards

Scattered throughout this book, we encountered numerous instances where the industry has not just acknowledged but celebrated Fiona's musical contributions with prestigious awards and nominations. This serves to underscore how her brilliance transcends both the hipster artistic culture and the mainstream ceremonial handshakes. So let's sing that praise one more time with feeling, compiling a comprehensive list of these accolades in one place.

All of her five albums have been recognised across nine Grammy Award nominations, twice up for the Best Female Rock Vocal Performance and twice up for Best Alternative Music Album. She has won three. In 1998, "Criminal" snatched the Best Female Rock Vocal Performance. In 2021, *Fetch the Bolt Cutters* earned two, one for Best Alternative Music Album, and one for Best Rock Performance with "Shameika".

Three MTV Video Music Award nominations led to two winnings: 1998's Best Cinematography for "Criminal" and 1997's Best New Artist in a Video's "Sleep to Dream", which resulted in that speech you might remember. Everyone remembers it.

Up for four Billboard Music Video Awards, she won the Best New Artist Clip for "Sleep to Dream" in 1997.

Beyond these high honours, there are several others worth noting, including:

- A VH1 Fashion Award (Most Stylish Music Video, "Criminal", 1997)
- Three Music Video Production Awards (Best Styling, "Criminal", 1998; Best Direction of a Female Artist and Best Hair, "O, Sailor", 2006)
- A Pollstar Concert Industry Awards (Club Tour of the Year, 1998)
- An ASCAP Pop Music Award (Most Performed Song, "Criminal", 1999)
- A California Music Award (Outstanding Female Vocalist, 2000)
- An Esky Music Award (Best Songbird, *Extraordinary Machine*, 2006)
- Six Rober Awards Music Poll Awards (Best Songwriter and Return of the Year, 2012; Best Female Artist, Songwriter of the Year, Album of the Year (*Fetch the Bolt Cutters*), and Song of the Year ("I Want You to Love Me"), 2020)
- A Daily Californian Art Award (Best Alternative Album, *Fetch the Bolt Cutters*, 2020)
- A Gold Derby Music Award (Best Rock/Alternative Artist, 2021)

Of course, we could go on with facts like how Reader's Poll voted her the Best Female Performer in 1998 or when Rolling Stone placed Apple as the 111th Greatest Singer of All Time in 2023, but we have to stop somewhere.

8.9.
Impact

To conclude this biography, we must ask ourselves: how does one accurately measure the success of an artist? Is it the awards they win, as documented above? Or is it instead their impact on the people of the world, an influence that amplifies through the echoes of other minds, permanently stitched into the DNA of human creativity?

Whatever your thoughts, Fiona has left an enduring mark on our culture, through the students of her music and the references of her name throughout other forms of media. This section will cover some of the more obvious examples where Fiona extends far beyond herself.

Cultural References

In Season 2, Episode 8 of *Sex and The City*, Steve asks Miranda to stay with him at the bar. Otherwise, he'll have to "listen to those NYU kids with the Amstel Lights discuss Fiona Apple."

Season 4, Episode 6 of *Buffy the Vampire Slayer*, Buffy compares the Veruca character to Fiona Apple. Unfavourably, at that! Boo!

Season 2, Episode 5 of *Girls*, Hannah relates a fake Fiona quote to herself.

"Okay, I read this article about Fiona Apple in New York Magazine where she said, 'Oh, everybody acts like I'm nuts. I'm not nuts. I just want to feel it all.' It's like, that's what I'm like. I just want to feel it all." [197]

– Hannah from Girls

Not only was a wicked cover of "Criminal" used in the Season 6 trailer for *Orange is the New Black*, but in Season 2, Boo was asked who she hopes is waiting for her on the outside of jail. She responds, "Fiona Apple in the 'Criminal' video."

Yet perhaps the strangest medium where you'll find Fiona references is in the animated world, for example, in South Park, Season 1 Episode 12 (*Mecha-Streisand*). Here, Barbra Streisand asks, "You know who I am, don't you?" to which Officer Barbrady replies, "Well, you ain't Fiona Apple, and if you ain't Fiona Apple, I don't give a rat's ass."

Of course, The Simpsons did it too. In Episode 7 of Season 30 (*Werking Mom*) we meet a drag queen whose stage name is hilariously Fiona Adam's Apple.

Family Guy took it to the next level. In Season 12, Episode 19 (*Meg Stinks!*), Peter and Meg Griffin go Fiona Apple picking. But that is nothing compared to Season 10, Episode

9 (*Grumpy Old Man*), when Joe Swanson performs his own unsettling cover version of the "Criminal" video.

Still, Bob's Burgers wins the game with Season 10, Episodes 4 (*Pig Trouble in Little Tina*). And we're not talking about when Gene Belcher dressed up as "Fiona Apple's saucy aunt, Fiona Applesauce", for Halloween. Instead, it's all about the end credits, where Fiona herself performs a pro-vegan song written for the episode.

"The writer of the episode, my co-show-runner, Nora Smith, wrote both the Fiona Applesauce joke and the 'Pig Trouble' song. I had been introduced to Fiona over email about a year ago and so I saw an opportunity to try and convince her to lend us her voice. She had previously said nice things about Bob's and even tossed out some deep cut references, so I was cautiously optimistic that she would say yes." [198]

– Loren Bouchard, Creator of Bob's Burgers

Artistic Influence and Praise
(feat. Kanye West, Lady Gaga, and Quentin Tarantino)

There is no end to other artists who bow to the ground Fiona walks on, but there are several individuals and quotes which stand taller.

Perhaps the most entertaining was the back-and-forth love between (early) Fiona and (early) Kanye West, with Apple interviewing West in 2005. Kanye did not restrain himself, gushing praise onto Fiona's debut as an inspiration for his second studio album, *Late Registration*.

"Now, when I listen to your shit, I hear similarities. I actually wanted to work with [Jon Brion] so I could be like the rap version of you. That was one of my main goals. The albums that inspired me for Late Registration were your first one, Tidal, and Portishead's Dummy. But especially your lyrics and how you sing." [199]

– Kanye West

When Kanye expressed his support for Trump, Fiona responded in 2018 with the following message:

"Alright, I'm not sure if I should say anything but I'm going to say something any-

way, and I say it with love. Kanye... [Trump] doesn't care about you. He doesn't care about your ideas. He doesn't care about black people. And if you think he cares about black people, please tell me why you think that." [200]

– Fiona Apple

No matter, there's plenty more happy vibes elsewhere! Here's Fiona on Lenny Kravitz:

"I wasn't his girlfriend or anything like that. But he and a friend came to the studio one night and told me how good it sounded. I ended up talking to Lenny a lot. He was the first person I could sit next to. Literally, he'll never understand how much he helped me." [20]

– Fiona Apple

And here's Lady Gaga:

"[Fiona Apple is] a comfort [...] I just revelled in the way that girl is so herself." [201]

– Lady Gaga

And here's Quentin Tarantino:

"Fiona is the singer songwriter of her gener- ation [...] she's got such a gifted voice, and she's such a gifted performer, and such a gifted musician, and you could talk about her for days, and never even bring that up. Just talk about the writing, all right? And her words and her rhymes and her phrases and her microscope on herself and on, you know, the human heart." [202]

– Quentin Tarantino

And here's Missy Elliott:

"I love her I-don't-give-a-fuck attitude." [203]

– Missy Elliott

And here's Sky Ferreira:

"I clearly remember the first album I bought was Tidal by Fiona Apple. I was six [...] and it really stuck with me. I think that's why I became such a big fan of hers. I've always listened to her basically my entire life so I

think she is probably my number one musician for that reason. [The label] wanted to say she was sullen and moody and crazy. And she was frustrated with it. I think she kind of was like, never mind, I'm done here. I'm like going away for a second. That's what's cool about her. She'll release an album, be like, alright, here it is, and then go. But like the album's always good. It stays good." [204]

— Sky Ferreira

And here's Sharon Van Etten:

"The emotional rawness and visceral angst and honesty of Fiona Apple's music was first met by my teenage years, sharing a bedroom with my little sister — who so patiently studied for school as I tried to write, sing, and play guitar in a way I wasn't ready for yet. Fiona made me want to be a better player. She made me want to have something to say. Although music has always been an important outlet for me, I knew I hadn't lived like she had. Having no concept of age, I heard

her voice as experienced and wise and someone that I wanted to be or to know. I carried her with me." [205]

– Sharon Van Etten

And here's St. Vincent:

"She's a true freak of nature. That brain of
hers is really something." [206]

– St. Vincent

And here's Andrew Bird:

"You look at a song like 'Werewolf' and, like,
the craft here is really incredibly masterful.
And I just want to say that I think [Fiona
is] one of the greats." [207]

– Andrew Bird

Jack Antonoff (the mastermind producer behind Taylor Swift
and Lana Del Rey) has a pretty incredible story to tell:

"I had a friend, and his dad had some
low-level position at Viacom or something
when I was a real kid, like real young. He
won tickets, and he took me to that VMAs

when [Fiona] gave that speech. I ran up the aisle right before that speech. I had my autograph book, and I was like, 'Fiona?' And she was getting drunk, and she gave me a kiss, and someone snapped a picture. I was right there, right before [the speech] happened. It was the craziest thing ever." [208]

– Jack Antonoff

The names go on and on. The legendary Elvis Costello covered Fiona's "I Know." Katie Crutchfield of Waxahatchee had a photo of Fiona hanging in her studio to inspire her while she recorded. And Solange Knowles was the President of the Fiona Apple Fan Club growing up. So, with such an exhilarating following, how does Fiona feel about the current musical landscape?

"I was at the Grammys, and I didn't know who anyone was." [209]

– Fiona Apple

In fact, when NPR called her the "godmother of 2019" for influencing such stars as Billie Eilish and Lana Del Rey, Fiona could not really comment on who these women were.

"I don't really follow, uh, I don't. I feel bad. But I don't." [210]

– Fiona Apple

I guess that's what makes Fiona so special. She remains largely uninfluenced, especially by contemporary standards.

"I just don't really listen to music. I'm probably missing out, but I don't want to know what everybody else is doing. Nobody is strong enough to not be influenced. And I don't mean influenced by copying. I'd be influenced because I wouldn't want to do what someone else is doing. I want to be able to do whatever I feel like doing and not worry about anything." [7]

– Fiona Apple

"I'm very thrilled that other people can get something out of my songs, but I write them for myself." [20]

– Fiona Apple

Saving the World One Apple At a Time

"It's simple. If I end up writing songs that I want to record and sing, then I'll be doing this. But I don't want to do it just for the sake of doing it. I'm not going to go and try to write songs. It's got to be the other way around. If I don't feel like writing songs, I will not force myself to make an album. Just pull one out of my ass just so that I can continue to be in the spotlight or something. It doesn't always have to be my career. There's no law that says that I have to have this as my career my whole life." [211]

– Fiona Apple

By writing, performing, and even producing her own groundbreaking records, Fiona has already solidified herself as one of the most important artists on the planet. However, if there is any takeaway from this biography that is more crucial than her musical output, it would be her contribution to society as a whole. Coming up as the underdog with immense strain placed upon her, Fiona has used her voice not only to soar above her piano but also as a weapon to arm those who can only manage a whisper.

Joining Kim Gordon, Fleet Foxes, and TV on the Radio,

Fiona Apple lent her name to Noise For Now and Seeding Sovereignty's COVID-19 relief campaign in 2020, providing masks for indigenous communities.

In 2000, she wrote a letter to assist a boy fighting for his high school's gay-straight alliance. It read:

"All I know is I want my friends to be good people, and when my friends fall in love, I want them to fall in love with other good people. How can you go wrong with two people in love? If a good boy loves a good girl, good. If a good boy loves another good boy, good. And if a good girl loves the goodness in good boys and good girls, then all you have is more goodness, and goodness has nothing to do with sexual orientation." [100]

– Fiona Apple

Remember when she donated two years' worth of "Criminal" profits to assist refugees with basic necessities, immigration fees, and legal services?

Remember when she funded dog rescues, placing strays in foster homes?

Remember when she volunteered to do occupational therapy for kids at Green Chimneys?

Remember when she wrote protest songs for women's rights, such as "Tiny Hands" and "For Her"?

Remember when she acknowledged indigenous land on the back of the *Fetch the Bolt Cutters* album cover?

Remember when she loudly fought for the rights of transparent trials by associating her name with Courtwatch PG?

How do those who previously said nasty things about Fiona feel about her now? Here she is, someone who measurably uses their status for the greater good. Indeed, it is more difficult to dislike Fiona than ever before.

Because for those of us who are inspired by Fiona, we can live through her and release our true selves like a tsunami of authenticity.

We can manoeuvre our chess pieces to never bow from the pressure of others, even when they're bigger than us.

We can fashion our inner mechanics to reframe any negative experience into a lesson of inspiration.

We can accept the cyclic nature of our emotional wheels, allowing everything to pass in its correct time.

We can muster enough strength to shatter any chains that have the audacity to think they can hold us back.

And we can do so along the path that best suits our personal journey, our power coming in many shapes and flavours, but always willing to nourish the lives of others who need it the most.

Like an apple.

Yeah, just like an apple.

"If you don't have anything nice to say, don't say anything at all. But if you have something nice to say, say it! If everybody said all the nice things that they had to say, then wouldn't it be a better place?" [212]

— Fiona Apple

Author Note

Thank you for reading my book! It was such a pleasure to dedicate the many months of research required to writing this biography because I love Fiona Apple and I love writing! In fact, I love writing so much that I quit my job in 2022 to dedicate myself to being a full-time book author. Eek!

Some people say I'm crazy. Others say I'm brave, which is probably a polite word for crazy. My dad used to say that writing a best-selling book is a one-in-a-million chance. I told him I'd just have to write a million books then.

I'm not claiming that my Fiona biography will skyrocket me to fame, but if it shoves a spoon of food into my mouth and allows me to pen my next project without worry, that would be the dream coming true right there! And that is where you come in.

Amazon's algorithm is an extremely intelligent beast that judges authors' products based on many factors. But inarguably, our most significant power comes from **verified reviews**. So when you take a few minutes to tell the world what you thought of this book, the website wakes up and lifts the title to higher eyes, feeding itself in the process. The author has no control over this side of the deal. It entirely relies on you!

Hence, please consider reviewing this Fiona Apple biography and help me work another day. You wouldn't believe the difference a single rating makes, and I read every one of them.

You can do so at **mybook.to/fionaapple**

Thank you again so very much!

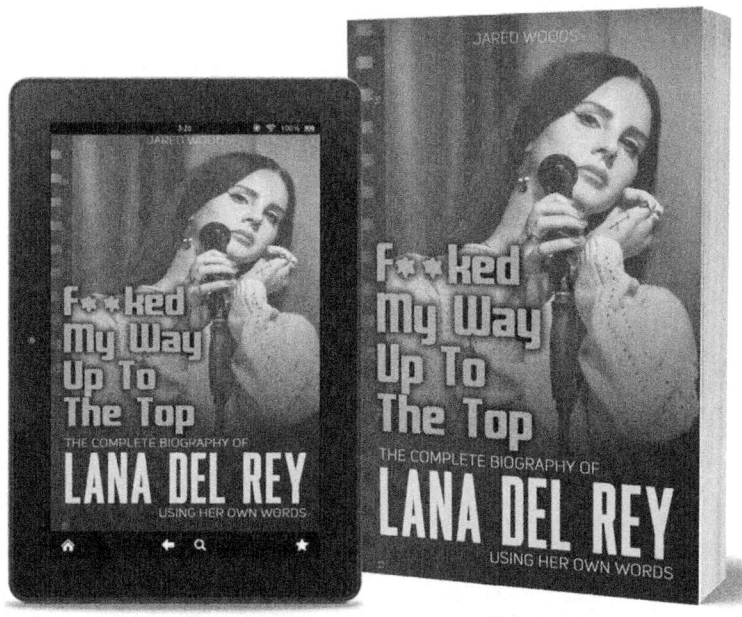

About the Author

Born in South Africa and now homeless as a nomadic something or other, Jared Woods does whatever he wants. His scriptwriting for the YouTube channel *Pencilmation* has been viewed by billions of people, with scripts surpassing the 100 million mark. An additional million-plus viewers have enjoyed his blog, *Juice Nothing*.

When a Song Ends in a Minor Key is the second biography in Jared's *"In Her Own Words"* series. The first is the phenomenally popular Lana Del Rey book, *F**ked My Way Up To The Top*, which is also available right now. His other publications include the relationship self-help books *Heartbreak Sucks! How to Get Over Your Breakup in 30 Days* (2021) and *Swiping Right* (2023), as well as his collection of dark short stories, *Licking the Bottom of the Love Jar* (2023). But most importantly, we have Jared's own religious scripture, the *Janthopoyism Bible* (2022). Get that first.

Further creative projects include his one-panel Instagram comic *#legobiscuits*, his solo music under the name *Coming Down Happy*, his "singing" for the band *Sectlinefor*, and his film production called *Definitely Not a Cry For Help* which is already partially on YouTube.

Support Jared on Patreon.com/legotrip
Visit Jared at JaredWoodsSavedMyLife.com
Follow Jared on Instagram, Twitter, Facebook, and Threads
@legotrip

Other Books by Jared Woods

- F**ked My Way Up to the Top: The Complete Biography of Lana Del Rey (2023)
- Janthopoyism Bible (2022)
- Licking the Bottom of the Love Jar (2023)
- Heartbreak Sucks! How to Get Over Your Breakup in 30 Days (2021)
- Swiping Right (2023)
- The 250 Best Albums of the Decade (2010 - 2019) (2019)

when
a song
ends in a
minor key

THE COMPLETE BIOGRAPHY OF

FIONA APPLE

USING HER OWN WORDS

by jared woods

References

[1] - https://www.newyorker.com/magazine/2020/03/23/fiona-apples-art-of-radical-sensitivity
[2] - https://youtu.be/qrAkzlld_Ts?si=QZGp9BVgMvOtSewu&t=1984
[3] - https://youtu.be/qrAkzlld_Ts?si=JEygHLz6tvW_bpEh&t=2168
[4] - https://youtu.be/qrAkzlld_Ts?si=C4LigQ-di1Jl6qM6&t=1835
[5] - https://www.youtube.com/watch?v=qrAkzlld_Ts&t=2086s
[6] - https://atlanticcityweekly.com/arts_and_entertainment/fiona-apple-interview-new-album-idler-wheel-slated-for-summer/article_70c54b01-60d1-590b-ae57-7d327added0a.html
[7] - https://pitchfork.com/features/interview/8853-fiona-apple
[8] - https://www.vulture.com/2012/06/hiding-out-with-fiona-apple-musical-hermit.html
[9] - https://www.interviewmagazine.com/music/fiona-apple-1
[10] - https://www.youtube.com/watch?v=b9kbKyW6MAU&t=224s
[11] - http://www.neverisapromise.com/interviews/Q300.html
[12] - http://sfj.abstractdynamics.org/archives/006509.html
[13] - https://pitchfork.com/news/46735-fiona-apple-interview-outtakes
[14] - https://youtu.be/u_ntl8ZE0V0?si=BmJAoof6UT_4jtju&t=175
[15] - https://youtu.be/kVnenNyaiY4?si=IWKc9NM5-3JJWy7X&t=256
[16] - https://pitchfork.com/features/article/fiona-apple-shameika-fetch-the-bolt-cutters-interview
[17] - https://www.youtube.com/watch?v=qrAkzlld_Ts&t=3815s
[18] - https://www.latimes.com/archives/la-xpm-1997-oct-05-ca-39318-story.html
[19] - https://www.vulture.com/2020/04/fiona-apple-fetch-the-bolt-cutters.html
[20] - https://www.rollingstone.com/feature/fiona-the-caged-bird-sings-244221
[21] - Q Magazine (March 2000). "Hard Core Pawn"
[22] - https://www.elephantjournal.com/2020/02/10-quotes-from-rock-and-rolls-feminist-badass-fiona-apple-billy-manas/
[23] - http://www.neverisapromise.com/interviews/Interview97.html
[24] - https://www.spin.com/featured/fiona-apple-tidal-november-1997-cover-story-girl-trouble
[25] - https://www.youtube.com/watch?v=BpYkbeU7Q2U&t=1817s
[26] - https://youtu.be/kVnenNyaiY4?si=6f1RJoXJHG3HGvVo&t=474
[27] - https://youtu.be/kVnenNyaiY4?si=9HZMQ3dz5hi7aDh-&t=552
[28] - https://youtu.be/qrAkzlld_Ts?si=6fIxA7JmOykp0M1B&t=3259
[29] - https://www.angelfire.com/zine2/pamela/famous.html
[30] - https://www.stereogum.com/2081479/fiona-apple-fetch-the-bolt-cutters-interview/news/
[31] - https://www.youtube.com/watch?v=qrAkzlld_Ts&t=2396s
[32] - https://youtu.be/qrAkzlld_Ts?si=JaxzO8yZWAT-oAS6&t=2300
[33] - https://youtu.be/qrAkzlld_Ts?si=XNuZ-nomTgG-gHzv&t=3968

[34] - https://youtu.be/tVwC9MyUuqs?si=fTNprd-09ToZpGCU&t=305

[35] - https://youtu.be/b-DbWyLAQ2w?si=B4HJ8CwDO4d_lyh_&t=65

[36] - https://www.youtube.com/watch?v=CaNqzEuRR6Q

[37] - http://www.neverisapromise.com/articles/aPhillyI1199.html

[38] - https://youtu.be/BpYkbeU7Q2U?si=_UhgFfJ8Cn1c0NM3&t=2155

[39] - https://youtu.be/b-DbWyLAQ2w?si=NTkhcB4l3iksPgJE&t=80

[40] - https://youtu.be/BpYkbeU7Q2U?si=saZZ8jq97Ln70G9f&t=3910

[41] - https://www.youtube.com/watch?v=b-DbWyLAQ2w

[42] - https://youtu.be/b-DbWyLAQ2w?si=CePcX07J2vdwmmcE&t=226

[43] - https://www.spin.com/2019/11/fiona-apple-when-the-pawn-interview

[44] - https://youtu.be/hx6hqM0ZqY4?si=4D0VRTB1dCa4JLU4&t=65

[45] - https://pitchfork.com/features/cover-story/fiona-apple-interview/

[46] - http://www.neverisapromise.com/interviews/DetailsJul97.html

[47] - https://www.youtube.com/watch?v=BpYkbeU7Q2U&t=849s

[48] - https://youtu.be/hx6hqM0ZqY4?si=1_AfuD6HuKXWPSS4&t=174

[49] - https://traceypepper.com/past-writing/journalism/fiona-apple

[50] - https://www.youtube.com/watch?v=4ah51vQfRL8

[51] - https://youtu.be/BpYkbeU7Q2U?si=WqNLx15x3SSKsAux&t=332

[52] - https://www.youtube.com/watch?v=BpYkbeU7Q2U&t=550s

[53] - https://youtu.be/G7YTv67Bg7E?si=zFIBXjIdVcl1ijZW&t=232

[54] - https://www.youtube.com/watch?v=hx6hqM0ZqY4

[55] - https://www.youtube.com/watch?v=b9kbKyW6MAU&t=319s

[56] - https://youtu.be/G7YTv67Bg7E?si=Kb1Sqr8au0ImOGt8&t=278

[57] - https://www.nickiswift.com/1039740/the-untold-truth-of-fiona-apple/

[58] - https://thevinylfactory.com/news/fiona-apple-debut-album-tidal-vinyl

[59] - https://www.youtube.com/watch?v=G7YTv67Bg7E&t=297s

[60] - https://www.youtube.com/watch?v=1pjIf5smBTs

[61] - https://albumism.com/features/tribute-celebrating-25-years-of-fiona-apple-tidal

[62] - https://www.halfmystic.com/blog/spread-like-strawberries

[63] - https://www.washingtonpost.com/entertainment/music/fiona-apple-tidal-anniversary/2021/07/21/47a355b4-e9ac-11eb-8950-d73b3e93ff7f_story.html

[64] - https://www.today.com/popculture/loyal-fans-helped-free-fiona-apple-s-cd-wbna9601227

[65] - Fiona Apple: The NUVO Interview, April, 1997

[66] - https://www.mtv.com/news/22rf74/kanye-west-twitter-2-2

[67]   -   https://archive.ph/20130201133719/http://www.rollingstone.com/music/news/macy-gray-sings-metallica-radiohead-and-more-on-covered-20120207/acceptance-speech-0937237

[68] - https://www.mtv.com/news/52qefg/fiona-apple-tidal-20-years

[69] - https://www.youtube.com/watch?v=QpVnUQd_K78

[70] - https://archive.ph/20190925171107/https://www.vulture.com/2019/09/fiona-apple-is-still-calling-bullshit.html#selection-3477.0-3477.420

[71] - https://archive.ph/20190925171107/https://www.vulture.com/2019/09/fiona-apple-is-still-calling-bullshit.html#selection-2079.3-2079.112

[72] - https://youtu.be/kVnenNyaiY4?si=PfZ9pIZbgiVH6qhD&t=781

[73] - https://books.google.ch/books?id=9CwEAAAAMBAJ&lpg=PA1&hl=de&pg=PT25#v=onepage&q&f=false

[74] - https://youtu.be/dCFHs-1wzpo?si=Nikp2fjm8Nm-fp9D&t=43

[75] - https://www.youtube.com/watch?v=qrAkzlld_Ts&t=4210s

[76] - https://www.youtube.com/watch?v=BpYkbeU7Q2U&t=956s

[77] - https://youtu.be/qrAkzlld_Ts?si=bXOf2W1l9oByG1ex&t=924

[78] - https://youtu.be/G7YTv67Bg7E?si=SIOcwBQmMSiIfxYr&t=346

[79] - https://www.nytimes.com/1997/01/05/arts/a-message-far-less-pretty-than-the-face.html

[80] - https://www.sfgate.com/music/popquiz/article/pop-quiz-q-a-with-fiona-apple-2819276.php

[81] - https://www.youtube.com/watch?v=G7YTv67Bg7E

[82] - https://youtu.be/b-DbWyLAQ2w?si=soY6zdN0zhDhOsXQ&t=186

[83] - https://www.youtube.com/watch?v=SFWO_CiD8nA
[84] - https://youtu.be/G7YTv67Bg7E?si=F0wNIHke8QThmKnN&t=815
[85] - https://www.washingtonpost.com/wp-srv/WPcap/1999-11/28/003r-112899-idx.html
[86] - https://www.notablebiographies.com/newsmakers2/2006-A-Ec/Apple-Fiona.html
[87] - https://youtu.be/b-DbWyLAQ2w?si=FieTLnDM4_y3E_3G&t=148
[88] - https://archive.ph/20190925171107/https://www.vulture.com/2019/09/fiona-apple-is-still-calling-bullshit.html#selection-2921.44-2927.360
[89] - https://www.theguardian.com/music/2020/dec/18/fiona-apple-i-finally-believed-myself-it-felt-great
[90] - https://youtu.be/kVnenNyaiY4?si=WT90Q4MvRGlhlf5z&t=129
[91] - http://www.neverisapromise.com/interviews/Tribeca.html
[92] - https://www.youtube.com/watch?v=VvlOFPAfYIM
[93] - https://www.youtube.com/watch?v=hoO1tvpTaio
[94] - https://www.youtube.com/watch?v=PXDji4guESc
[95] - https://youtu.be/xyOMvd1zt4g?si=aGpiexN-7bXnC8pk&t=434
[96] - https://atwoodmagazine.com/fawp-fiona-apple-when-the-pawn-album-review-24-year-anniversary
[97] - https://youtu.be/qrAkzlld_Ts?si=Eb6GTAIKzl7uX3Hl&t=3458
[98] - https://youtu.be/kVnenNyaiY4?si=iUrUJSxcMgPoXoCu&t=349
[99] - https://www.rollingstone.com/music/music-news/fiona-apple-addresses-heckling-outburst-98702
[100] - https://web.archive.org/web/20120603033544/http://www.blackbookmag.com/music/the-long-and-winding-road-that-leads-to-fiona-apple-1.49114
[101] - https://www.instyle.com/news/tbt-fiona-apple-david-blaine-relationship
[102] - https://archive.org/details/the-long-hard-road-out-of-hell-by-marilyn-manson-and-neil-strauss/page/188/mode/2up?q=fiona
[103] - https://www.kerrang.com/dave-navarro-once-wrote-fiona-apple-a-love-letter-in-his-own-blood
[104] - https://youtu.be/YNlVPl73rdQ?si=K9J4iDlU2LOam3Kz&t=69
[105] - https://youtu.be/kVnenNyaiY4?si=fZd5xlslzZvU8zoE&t=372
[106] - https://www.youtube.com/watch?v=ToCvvLNH8X0
[107] - https://www.youtube.com/watch?v=qrAkzlld_Ts&t=3141s
[108] - https://www.youtube.com/watch?v=BpYkbeU7Q2U&t=2115s
[109] - https://youtu.be/kVnenNyaiY4?si=2tNm2tcjoUHFQ6EB&t=878
[110] - https://americansongwriter.com/jon-brion-on-producing-fiona-apple
[111] - http://www.neverisapromise.com/interviews/PS800.html
[112] - http://www.neverisapromise.com/interviews/WallofSound1199.htm
[113] - https://www.smackmedia.ca/deep-cuts/when-the-pawn
[114] - https://www.vinylmeplease.com/blogs/magazine/when-the-pawn-liner-notes-1
[115] - https://www.rollingstone.com/music/music-news/qa-fiona-apple-109396/
[116] - https://youtu.be/1rNGUVFTY50?si=Fvo5d_amzMJ-xW_O&t=65
[117] - http://www.neverisapromise.com/articles/vh1oct99.htm
[118] - https://youtu.be/qrAkzlld_Ts?si=O0ungTznzB6vBBLr&t=4063
[119] - http://www.neverisapromise.com/articles/aUSA1199.htm
[120] - https://www.youtube.com/watch?v=BpYkbeU7Q2U&t=4846s
[121] - https://www.youtube.com/watch?v=G7YTv67Bg7E&t=601s
[122] - https://youtu.be/qrAkzlld_Ts?si=HNYxr3o5TQ4UHEAv&t=4470
[123] - https://www.spin.com/2012/05/fiona-apples-return-idle-no-more/3/
[124] - https://youtu.be/xdCEFkBwYU0?si=aYF93-cFYIR72tm9&t=138
[125] - https://youtu.be/BpYkbeU7Q2U?si=gtzlTpujAv9iUxxb&t=3131
[126] - https://youtu.be/b9kbKyW6MAU?si=yl__BsPy_GWHXuet&t=125
[127] - https://youtu.be/BpYkbeU7Q2U?si=xeTHl7HZjpiUJqmg&t=4165
[128] - https://youtu.be/BpYkbeU7Q2U?si=XnLhHWbp5ltuQMFp&t=4289
[129] - https://youtu.be/b-DbWyLAQ2w?si=F3r0xm8mahSAm2eZ&t=226
[130] - https://youtu.be/BpYkbeU7Q2U?si=Ar1xR03lwk51rwD-&t=3787

[131] - https://faroutmagazine.co.uk/johnny-cash-fiona-apple-cover-bridge-over-troubled-water/
[132] - https://web.archive.org/web/20060509153700/http://www.rollingstone.com/artists/theroots/articles/story/7595844/fiona_talks_machine
[133] - https://youtu.be/ogpbudycgl8?si=EMQ8Dk5gLGEgMUwR&t=205
[134] - https://youtu.be/BpYkbeU7Q2U?si=1f1PgkTYjkH8VHLH&t=3486
[135] - https://www.jimdero.com/News2005/FionaAppleFeatureDec2.htm
[136] - https://www.mtv.com/news/217s1p/whatever-happened-to-fiona-apple-online-campaign-tries-to-find-out
[137] - https://youtu.be/zIu7nEYORU4?si=aiBU4WhcyBXDohow&t=374
[138] - https://youtu.be/G7YTv67Bg7E?si=yDQi_pp4gDDLaNmz&t=1204
[139] - https://www.billboard.com/music/music-news/fiona-fashions-a-different-machine-61771/
[140] - https://youtu.be/xyOMvd1zt4g?si=C2qt9Ko1vwfXAPPP&t=354
[141] - https://youtu.be/YlZ9mFUW9i4?si=HDPveOsdG8WFrYte&t=42
[142] - https://www.latimes.com/entertainment/la-xpm-2012-jun-24-la-ca-fiona-apple-20120624-story.html
[143] - https://youtu.be/CV2yrhM2juQ?si=Qa1O5RPdxxWU-Kxq&t=390
[144] - https://www.eastbaytimes.com/2006/06/23/fiona-apples-back-with-extraordinary-machine
[145] - https://www.mtv.com/news/5j76io/fiona-apple-haunts-ocean-liner-in-new-clip-may-release-alternate-version-of-new-lp
[146] - https://www.mtv.com/news/q80xav/if-you-think-fiona-grew-a-beard-youre-not-paying-attention
[147] - https://youtu.be/CaNqzEuRR6Q?si=fepirODAV0gApsiV&t=122
[148] - https://books.google.com.co/books?id=9VQ5UluNUkIC&pg=PA22&redir_esc=y#v=onepage&q&f=false
[149] - https://youtu.be/65eWgmm3ZrU?si=Q9nBJz_GfnASvp9A&t=184
[150] - https://www.youtube.com/watch?v=SV-ImEakMsM
[151] - https://en.wikipedia.org/wiki/Extraordinary_Machine
[152] - https://www.mtv.com/news/x33p0g/fiona-apples-long-delayed-lp-slotted-for-october-4-release
[153] - https://www.billboard.com/music/music-news/fiona-apple-the-billboard-cover-story-483015
[154] - https://www.youtube.com/watch?v=Kwi6q9FDzz8
[155] - https://youtu.be/q39k2zucBh4?si=cApWm7LrK6M3-5ct&t=204
[156] - https://youtu.be/qrAkzlld_Ts?si=EejK50PumFP0xA9-&t=1199
[157] - https://www.spin.com/2012/05/fiona-apples-return-idle-no-more/4/
[158] - https://www.nytimes.com/2012/06/03/arts/music/fiona-apples-new-album-the-idler-wheel.html
[159] - https://pitchfork.com/news/46795-video-fiona-apple-every-single-night
[160] - https://genius.com/a/fiona-apple-explains-why-she-refused-to-let-panic-at-the-disco-sample-her-on-miss-jackson/
[161] - https://www.rollingstone.com/music/music-news/fiona-apple-lil-nas-x-891584
[162] - https://www.npr.org/transcripts/154577052?storyId=154577052?storyId=154577052
[163] - https://youtu.be/e6jnHA-vjPA?si=4HGmC73WVHYsudRF&t=144
[164] - https://www.youtube.com/watch?v=a46FKCXY0l4&t=109s
[165] - https://youtu.be/4xoA-QcBj0M?si=fUbSzUhidBRxMLyD&t=374
[166] - https://www.billboard.com/music/music-news/fiona-apple-banked-on-buzz-to-build-anticipation-for-new-release-1093344
[167] - https://newsfeed.time.com/2012/11/21/in-heartbreaking-handwritten-letter-fiona-apple-cancels-tour-to-be-with-dying-dog/#:~:text=The%2035%2Dyear%2Dold%20singer,decision%20in%20heart%2Dwrenching%20detail
[168] - https://www.esquire.com/entertainment/music/a31675518/fiona-apple-quit-cocaine-quentin-tarantino-paul-thomoas-anderson
[169] - https://www.youtube.com/watch?v=RWhI4MU2tMs
[170] - https://youtu.be/CV2yrhM2juQ?si=bHomyIl1FdZQbSwC&t=403
[171] - https://pitchfork.com/features/interview/9011-judd-apatow
[172] - https://pitchfork.com/features/update/9234-update-fiona-apple

[173] - *https://www.stereogum.com/1709454/hear-fiona-apples-container-the-theme-to-showtimes-the-affair/news/*

[174] - *https://www.stereogum.com/2150412/shirley-manson-garbage-no-gods-no-masters-fiona-apple-elijah-wood-kathleen-hanna/interviews/weve-got-a-file-on-you*

[175] - *https://variety.com/2018/music/news/shirley-manson-on-her-duet-with-fiona-apple-kneel-portnow-1202692618*

[176] - *https://www.stereogum.com/2081479/fiona-apple-fetch-the-bolt-cutters-interview/news*

[177] - *https://youtu.be/G7YTv67Bg7E?si=K-hPptoD6KVC3VGA&t=1558*

[178] - *https://www.npr.org/2020/04/22/841401198/fetch-your-tool-of-liberation-fiona-apple-on-setting-herself-free*

[179] - *https://pitchfork.com/features/cover-story/fiona-apple-interview*

[180] - *https://youtu.be/G7YTv67Bg7E?si=dveIV6ClIk-ZlCVH&t=1663*

[181] - *https://www.ibtimes.com/fiona-apple-opens-about-her-relationship-her-exes-women-she-crossed-2960635*

[182] - *https://youtu.be/G7YTv67Bg7E?si=5KHtmtZy1X762uxV&t=1801*

[183] - *https://www.youtube.com/watch?v=G7YTv67Bg7E&t=1618s*

[184] - *https://youtu.be/G7YTv67Bg7E?si=oTSzoooXRfj99Smx&t=1751*

[185] - *https://www.nbcwashington.com/news/local/fiona-apples-shameika-lives-in-virginia-is-amazed-by-song/2521763*

[186] - *https://pitchfork.com/features/article/fiona-apple-shameika-fetch-the-bolt-cutters-interview*

[187] - *https://www.youtube.com/watch?v=rDI7U0sBX-k*

[188] - *https://youtu.be/BpYkbeU7Q2U?si=NaWph9DSnjEG312p&t=3871*

[189] - *https://www.youtube.com/watch?v=o7r7ZQT_pHk*

[190] - *https://www.youtube.com/watch?v=94WXCgKuOws*

[191] - *https://dcist.com/story/22/10/25/fiona-apple-calls-out-prince-georges-county-courts-for-cutting-access-to-remote-hearings*

[192] - *https://twitter.com/ScottHech/status/1584525192159580163*

[193] - *https://www.instagram.com/p/CMYy25aJjcr/*

[194] - *https://dcist.com/story/21/03/30/fiona-apple-pg-county-courtwatching-group-membership-skyrocketed/*

[195] - *https://www.discourseblog.com/p/fiona-apples-court-watch-advocacy*

[196] - *https://www.youtube.com/watch?v=39TqiyErdnY*

[197] - *https://www.tiktok.com/@linnabag/video/7178425496135372038*

[198] - *https://www.livekindly.com/fiona-apple-pig-song-bobs-burgers*

[199] - *https://fionaapplerocks.tumblr.com/post/64613120297/fiona-apple-interviews-kanye-west-oct-2005*

[200] - *https://www.youtube.com/watch?v=pxkaDfK-q7o*

[201] - *https://consequence.net/2021/07/fiona-apple-tidal-anniversary-essay*

[202] - *https://www.youtube.com/watch?v=Cpae7plbvBo*

[203] - *https://www.spin.com/2012/05/fiona-apples-return-idle-no-more/2/*

[204] - *https://www.youtube.com/watch?v=g0712EFVOvQ*

[205] - *https://consequence.net/2021/04/fiona-apple-cover-sharon-van-etten-love-more-stream*

[206] - *https://www.bbc.co.uk/programmes/articles/3w469zJK5gKP5lJ5tNRFf3D/bjork-st-vincent-and-more-on-the-trailblazing-women-whose-music-you-need-to-hear*

[207] - *https://youtu.be/e6jnHA-vjPA?si=LiexxPzj-4NbXJiB&t=601*

[208] - *https://www.instagram.com/pitchfork/reel/C4THQZ4siXg*

[209] - *https://youtu.be/1rNGUVFTY50?si=oLuD6jKLFNgohqyD&t=135*

[210] - *https://archive.ph/20190925171107/https://www.vulture.com/2019/09/fiona-apple-is-still-calling-bullshit.html#selection-3715.0-3715.60*

[211] - *https://youtu.be/qrAkzlld_Ts?si=Pe29AXfNKtoN14JU&t=1429*

[212] - *https://youtu.be/BpYkbeU7Q2U?si=3VT7LYTAEcv-OylY&t=4129*

When a Song Ends in a Minor Key:
The Complete Biography of Fiona Apple Using Her Own Words
by Jared Woods
co-editing by Milz Dechnik
cover photo by Photo12
published by The Goat's Nest Publishing
ISBN 9798332405389
ASIN B0D821KMH7
JaredWoodsSavedMyLife.com

Printed in Great Britain
by Amazon